SCHOOL OF
ORIENTAL AND AFRICAN STUDIES
UNIVERSITY OF LONDON

London Oriental Bibliographies
Volume 3

LONDON ORIENTAL BIBLIOGRAPHIES · VOLUME 3

BIBLIOGRAPHY OF MALAY AND ARABIC PERIODICALS

PUBLISHED IN THE STRAITS SETTLEMENTS AND PENINSULAR MALAY STATES

1876—1941

WITH AN ANNOTATED UNION LIST
OF HOLDINGS IN
MALAYSIA, SINGAPORE AND
THE UNITED KINGDOM

BY

WILLIAM R. ROFF

Columbia University, New York

LONDON
OXFORD UNIVERSITY PRESS
1972

Oxford University Press, Ely House, London W. 1

GLASGOW NEW YORK TORONTO MELBOURNE WELLINGTON
CAPE TOWN IBADAN NAIROBI DAR ES SALAAM LUSAKA ADDIS ABABA
DELHI BOMBAY CALCUTTA MADRAS KARACHI LAHORE DACCA
KUALA LUMPUR SINGAPORE HONG KONG TOKYO

ISBN 0 19 713572 2

© *W. R. Roff, 1972*

*Printed in Great Britain
at the University Press, Oxford
by Vivian Ridler
Printer to the University*

CONTENTS

ACKNOWLEDGEMENTS

THE passage of time increases rather than diminishes one's sense of indebtedness to others. The preparation of the present bibliography has benefited greatly from the continued co-operation of those who helped me with my *Guide to Malay Periodicals* in 1961 and were therein acknowledged. To them I should like to add Dato' Alwi Jantan, Director of the Arkib Negara Malaysia, and his staff (especially Che' Zakiah Hanum); Mr. Beda Lim, Librarian of the University of Malaya, and his staff (especially Mr. Eddie Yeoh); Mrs. Hedwig Anuar, Director of the National Library and Archives in Singapore, and her staff; Sayyid Ahmad b. Ali, Librarian of the Dewan Bahasa dan Pustaka in Kuala Lumpur, and Inche Abdul Samad b. Ahmad of the Dewan's editorial staff; and Mr. J. H. Eisenegger, lately of the Department of Oriental Printed Books and Manuscripts of the British Museum.

This work is dedicated with affection and respect to the memory of the late Dato' Haji Ahmad b. Ismail, Dato' Lela Negara of Kelantan, who died in 1969 after a long life of service to periodical journalism and Malay letters.

I am glad to acknowledge the assistance given by the Publications Committee of the School of Oriental and African Studies, University of London, which has met the full cost of production of this work.

W. R. R.

INTRODUCTION

SINCE my earlier *Guide to Malay Periodicals* was published in 1961, bibliographical knowledge of Malay (and Arabic) periodicals has been greatly enriched, titles have been added, holdings previously unknown have been newly listed or newly microfilmed, and some deposits have changed hands. Because of this, and because the *Guide* has been out of print for many years, a fresh attempt to present this material seemed desirable. Though the basic plan of the original *Guide* has been retained, opportunity has been taken to reorganize and expand the contents, to provide a much longer, analytical (and it is hoped more helpful) introduction to the Malay press of the time, and to offer some remarks on the present state of holdings.

In 1961 it was reported that 147 periodicals were known to have been published in the Malay language in the peninsular Malay states and the Straits Settlements between 1876 and 1941, with a further six published in English by Malays or devoted to Malay concerns. With the passage of time these figures have had to be revised and refined. We now know of 162 Malay-language periodicals during this period (including one in what is now East Malaysia), together with eight published in English by or for Malays and three published partly in Malay and partly in English (one of the latter partly also in Tamil). In addition to this basic 173 it is possible to list, for the sake of cultural and linguistic completeness, fifteen periodicals published in Arabic (all in Singapore, and all in the 1930s), and nine published in the Malay language by Christian missions for missionary purposes (again all in Singapore, two of them in the 1850s).

The first thing that must strike any student of the Malay press before the Second World War is its overwhelming concentration in two of the Straits Settlements—Singapore and Penang. The reasons for this are primarily economic and cultural. Both were large and wealthy cities with considerable populations not only of Malays but of Malay-literate Baba Chinese, Jawi Peranakan, and Arabs. As cities they were able to provide the printing presses and ancillary facilities needed to produce newspapers and journals, the intellectual stimulation characteristic of urban life, and a conveniently localized readership of some size. By contrast, the Malay population in the peninsular states was for the most part widely dispersed in difficult terrain, and often inaccessible not just to newspapers but to the education which alone could teach people to read and encourage them to take an interest in affairs beyond the village. It is therefore hardly surprising that of the 173 Malay periodical titles published between 1876 and 1941 no fewer than 104 appeared in Singapore or Penang (68 and 36 respectively), nor that of the 26 periodicals published during the first forty years of this period only four appeared in the peninsular states, all in Perak.[1] These figures draw attention, of course, to their corollary, namely that if only 26 papers appeared in the first forty years, no fewer than 147 did so in the remaining thirty-five years, of which 68, or close to half, were published in the peninsular states. Indeed, the history of the Malay press after the First World War is a history of continued accelera-tion, both in terms of new publications and in terms of reduction in the dis-parity between Singapore/Penang and the peninsular states. This, of course, is understandable, as increasing numbers of Malays in the peninsula became literate, became better off economically, and acquired an interest in reading, whether for information, self-improvement, or entertainment. Less im-mediately explicable, perhaps, until one thinks about the population figures (and even these do not tell the whole story) is that of the 68 peninsular periodicals appearing between 1917 and 1941, only 32 were published in the materially much more advanced Federated Malay States, compared with 36 in the 'underdeveloped' Unfederated States, mostly in Johore and Kelantan. When one recalls that in 1931 the literacy rate for Kelantan Malay males aged 15 and above was 8 per cent (compared, for example, with 62 per cent in urban Kuala Lumpur, 52 per cent in Perak, or 29 per cent in Johore), it is surely a matter for remark that this state alone gave birth to no fewer than twelve periodicals between 1917 and 1938.[2]

But statistics themselves, though seductive, mean little enough and often mislead. Much depends on what sorts of periodical we are talking about, how long-lasting or ephemeral, and how limited or extensive in circulation. It is therefore perhaps worth trying to discuss briefly some of the principal characteristics of the Malay press during the late nineteenth and early twentieth centuries in relation to major developments, to classes of publica-tion, and to particular periodicals of interest to the historian. What follows,

---

[1] A fifth, the official Malay version of the Perak *Government Gazette*, has been omitted from this calculation, though listed in the bibliography itself.

[2] The following table gives (a) the total Malay ('Malaysian') population of each of the peninsular states in 1931, (b) literacy percentages for over-15 Malay males, (c) the resulting population of literate Malay males over 15, and (d) the number of periodicals published in each state between 1876 and 1941. It should be emphasized that (c) can only be an approxi-mation.

State	(a)	(b)	(c)	(d)
Perak	272,546	52	41,901	18
Selangor	122,868	46	18,550	7*
Negri Sembilan	87,195	57	14,602	8
Pahang	111,122	35	10,748	0
Johore	234,422	29	22,102	21†
Kedah	286,262	22	19,257	3
Kelantan	330,774	8	7,963	12
Trengganu	164,564	8	3,932	3

* Includes one title previously published in Negri Sembilan.
† Includes three titles previously published in Singapore. Source for (a), (b), and (c): *British Malaya: A Report on the 1931 Census*, comp. by C. A. Vlieland, London, 1932.

it should be emphasized, does not pretend to be a history of Malay journalism. It is intended merely to make the contents of the *Bibliography* of greater practical use to scholars unfamiliar with the material.

The first phase

The most distinctive feature of Malay journalism in its early years, apart from its provenance, was its ethnically 'non-Malay' character, though for the most part non-Malay in a special and limited sense. The first periodical of any kind published in the Malay language was entitled, appropriately enough, *Jawi Peranakan*. It was founded by members of an association of Straits-born Muslims of part South Indian, part Malay descent and largely Malay culture—the community known, in fact, as Jawi Peranakan. It is important to recognize that the Jawi Peranakan thought of themselves very much as Malays, and in their papers identified entirely with Malay interests, speaking always of 'we Malays' or 'this Malay community' and primarily reporting Malay affairs. Of the seventeen periodical titles published between the appearance of *Jawi Peranakan* in 1876 and 1905 (a convenient 'first phase' of thirty years), a majority seems certainly to have had Jawi Peranakan sponsors and editors. It is convenient to discuss these seventeen papers systematically in terms of each of the three territories producing them—Singapore, Penang, and Perak.

Jawi Peranakan, besides being the first Malay newspaper, was also the longest lived prior to 1941, appearing for something like nineteen years until April 1895. Published weekly, it offered its readers general if brief coverage of foreign and local news (most of the former drawn from the English-language press) and frequent reports from elsewhere in the region—especially the peninsular states but also Java, Sumatra, and other parts of the archipelago. Though limited in size (folio, but seldom more than four pages in length) and consequently in editorial space, and somewhat self-abnegatory in political comment, it developed an identifiable style, performed real services of information, and remains useful to the historian interested not only in the Malayo-Muslims of late nineteenth-century Singapore but in the surrounding region. It was the first of seven papers to be published in Singapore before 1905, of which five form a group led by *Jawi Peranakan* itself. The next two of the five, *Nujumu'l-Fajar* and *Shamsu'l-Kamar*, had brief, possibly consecutive and associated lives in the late 1870s. There are no known holdings of either today, and they are in consequence of limited interest to scholars. In 1880 a fourth paper was started, *Sekola Melayu*, edited by the then editor of *Jawi Peranakan*, Munshi Mohd. Ali b. Ghulam al-Hindi, probably to provide additional reading matter in Malay schools. Like most of its contemporaries (except *Jawi Peranakan*, which imported movable type from England in 1877) *Sekola Melayu* was hand-lithographed on rather absorbent newsprint, and is now difficult to read. In general, *Sekola Melayu* provided less in the way of news or comment than its contemporary, *Jawi Peranakan*, though it should be said that it was not in any detectable sense a 'children's newspaper'. After the demise of *Jawi Peranakan* in 1895 there was a long period during which Singapore had no locally produced Malay paper, until in 1904 Munshi Mohd. Ali began to bring out *Taman Pengetahuan*, a direct successor, it may be supposed, to *Jawi Peranakan*. Though no holdings of *Taman Pengetahuan* exist, it is probable that it was similar to its precursor, and like *Jawi Peranakan* it was printed not lithographed.

The two remaining Singapore papers of these years are of interest as the first of a number of periodicals brought out in Malay by and primarily for the Baba (or Straits-born) Chinese, though they usually had a Malay audience as well. The *Straits Chinese Herald*, at once the first daily to be published at least partly in the Malay language and the first Malay paper to be printed in the roman script, appeared during the early part of 1891, but possibly not for longer than a few months. The paper contained news and editorials in English, with a varying amount translated into Malay. Of greater interest journalistically was the Singapore *Bintang Timor*, a wholly Malay-language paper published daily for nine months from July 1894 and then thrice-weekly for the last three months of its existence. Though appearing under the auspices of the Chinese Christian Association, *Bintang Timor*, under the editorship of the very able Song Ong Siang, was a straightforward daily newspaper without proselytizing tendencies, and an often provocative commentator on the local scene. It engaged in frequent journalistic controversy with its contemporary *Jawi Peranakan*, both ceasing publication at about the same time.

It is perhaps permissible here to digress briefly in order to draw attention to the remaining Straits Chinese papers which were to appear in later years. There were at least nine, possibly ten,[1] of which only those for which there are substantial holdings will be mentioned here. *Kabar Slalu* was a daily, published for four months in 1924; *Kabar Uchapan Baru*, published more or less weekly in both Malay and English, appeared between 1926 and 1930; *Perdagangan* was a commercial paper run by what may be assumed to have been an Indonesian Chinese company in Singapore from 1928; *Bintang Pranakan* was a weekly published for a few months in 1930-1; *The Story Teller* (not strictly a periodical at all, perhaps, but the publication in fortnightly serial parts of a Chinese romance) was published in 1934-5; and finally a journal entitled *Eastern Weekly Review*, which appeared in Malay and English for a time in 1925, may or may not have been published under Straits Chinese auspices. All the foregoing were published in Singapore, and all in the romanized script. Part of their present interest lies in the extent to which they may, perhaps, reflect a specifically Straits Chinese view of

[1] And perhaps an eleventh. An editorial in *Jawi Peranakan*, 23 Oct. 1893 (reprinted in Mohd. b. Dato' Muda, *Tarikh Surat Khabar* (Bukit Mertajam, 1940), pp. 93–4) refers to a new Baba Chinese paper entitled *Peranakan*, published in Singapore. No other reference has been discovered.

Malayan affairs, but they are of interest also linguistically (as many of their titles imply) for studies of that variant of the language known as 'Baba Malay'. It should be noted that several were very short lived, and it seems likely that the most profitable for further study may be *Kabar Slalu, Kabar Uchapan Baru,* and *Bintang Pranakan,* which in addition span crucial years for the Chinese community in Malaya, 1924–31.

Returning to the nineteenth century and to Penang, five periodicals were published there between 1876 and 1905,[1] all with mainly Jawi Peranakan editorial staffs. The first of these, *Tanjong Penegeri,* was also the first non-Baba Malay paper to publish as frequently as twice a week, in 1894–5. Like the two weeklies which succeeded it, *Pemimpin Warta* (1895–7) and *Lengkongan Bulan* (1900–1), it was a hand-lithographed, four-page folio newspaper, now rather difficult to read. Though the amount of local news and comment appearing in these papers is not great, they help the historian to fill the gap created by the break in newspaper publication in Singapore, between the cessation of *Jawi Peranakan* in 1895 and the starting of *Taman Pengetahuan* in 1904. In March 1900, the first printed (as distinct from lithographed) Penang paper began publication, the weekly *Bintang Timor,* but it failed after thirty issues and was replaced shortly thereafter by *Chahaya Pulau Pinang,* under the same Jawi Peranakan editor, Abdul Ghani b. Mohd. Kassim, but financed now by the Chinese-owned Criterion Press. *Chahaya Pulau Pinang,* which was to enjoy a much more healthy existence, ran for eight and a half years, until March 1908, thus becoming the most successful Penang paper (in these terms) until *Saudara* in the 1930s. Publishing at a time when interest was aroused in Malay and Islamic circles by the troubled affairs of the declining Ottoman empire, *Chahaya Pulau Pinang* reported regularly and at length on the Middle East, often translating portions from Egyptian and other newspapers. A sober and well-produced journal, it is for the historian particularly illustrative of changing interests and styles in Malay journalism.

The first paper to be published in any of the peninsular states was *Seri Perak,* in Taiping, which came out weekly for an uncertain but probably brief period from June 1893. In the absence of known holdings it is difficult to discover much about *Seri Perak,* but it seems likely that the editor was Haji Abdul Kadir b. Setia Raja, probably the first full Malay to run a Malay-language newspaper. *Seri Perak* appears to have been supported, if not owned, by the Pioneer Press, publisher of the English-language bi-weekly *Perak Pioneer* (though this paper did not itself start publication until 1894), the same firm also sponsoring *Seri Perak*'s successor in Taiping, *Jajahan Melayu. Jajahan Melayu,* which appeared in lithograph weekly from November

---

[1] E. W. Birch, 'The Vernacular Press in the Straits', *Journal of the Straits Branch, Royal Asiatic Society,* 4 (1880), p. 52, refers in addition to a Penang *Jawi Standard,* said to have been contemporaneous with *Jawi Peranakan* and *Shamsu'l-Kamar* (i.e. *c.* 1876–8), but no other reference has been found.

1896 to October 1897 (and possibly a little longer), contained, in the main, straits and peninsula news of a general kind, with some foreign reports and an uncertain proportion of local material. The remaining two peninsular papers of this period were also published in Perak, the weekly *Jambangan Warta* of Batu Gajah, in 1901 (of which nothing is known), and the monthly *Khizanah al-Ilmu* of Kuala Kangsar, in 1904. Concerning the latter, which may well have been the first self-improvement magazine (as distinct from newspaper) in Malay, little is known, though it is remarked by the author of *Tarikh Surat Khabar* that its contents belied its high-sounding title.

The second phase

The second phase of Malay journalism, the decade from 1906 to 1916, is marked by two phenomena, the rise of the major 'national' daily, and the appearance of serious religious journals of a reformist and influential kind. Apart from Baba Chinese papers, only seven periodicals were started during this period, none anywhere other than Singapore, but most were of some importance and continue to be of interest to scholars.

When *Utusan Melayu* was launched in November 1907 its only existing competitor was *Chahaya Pulau Pinang* (which stopped publication four months later), and for the next seven years *Utusan* was the only Malay newspaper regularly circulating in the Straits Settlements and the peninsula.[1] Though not at this time a daily, it appeared three times a week, a great deal more frequently than had any of its predecessors, and for the first time something like daily newspaper journalism became possible in Malay. Full advantage of this was taken by the paper's first editor, Mohd. Eunos b. Abdullah, who is often described as 'the father of Malay journalism' (though paternity is sometimes disputed). The paper was founded and owned by the proprietor and editor of the *Singapore Free Press*, William Makepeace, as a Malay edition of that paper. In fact, though it continued to rely heavily on the *Free Press*'s news services, it rapidly became a distinctive, and at its best a distinguished, paper on its own account. Like all its contemporaries, it was a four-page (later six-page) folio paper, and its editorial space was further limited by the device of repeating in romanized script on the back page (presumably for the benefit of Baba Chinese readers) the editorial and main news appearing in jawi script elsewhere. Despite these handicaps it developed into an excellent mirror of and commentator upon the times, contained a great deal more local news than any of its predecessors, and ran a useful and lively correspondence column. It became a daily in September 1915. Though the paper ran into difficulties towards the end of its career, and finally foundered in 1921, it remains an invaluable guide to the years during which it appeared, and it is fortunate that extant holdings are reasonably complete.

[1] Nothing at all is known of the fortnightly *Al-Watan*, which was probably not a 'news' paper, and may even have been in Arabic.

The thrice-weekly *Utusan Melayu* was joined in August 1914 by a new Malay daily, *Lembaga Melayu*, owned and published by the simultaneously established Singapore English-language paper, *Malaya Tribune*, and edited by Mohd. Eunos b. Abdullah, who was to remain there for seventeen years until the paper ceased publication at the end of 1931. *Lembaga Melayu* started with limited aims, as a single news sheet containing translations of overseas news from the agency services of the *Tribune*, and though it expanded soon after this to the standard four-page folio size, it did not for many years (largely, no doubt, because of pressure of war news) lose its slightly lifeless air of translated telegramese. In the 1920s, however, when it was the only Malay daily in circulation (after the demise of *Utusan*), it appears to have contained a greater proportion of local news and comment, and to have participated much more fully in Malay causes—something in which Mohd. Eunos's dual role as a municipal commissioner and as the first Malay member of the Straits Settlements Legislative Council must have assisted. Little beyond crude figures is now discoverable about the circulation of either *Utusan Melayu* or *Lembaga Melayu*,[1] but it is clear that they enjoyed a considerable audience in the Straits Settlements and at least the towns of the peninsular states as Malay literacy grew and political questions affecting Malays came to the fore. It was the pressing nature of the latter, perhaps, which led, even if indirectly, to the decline and disappearance of *Lembaga Melayu* in 1931. Almost exactly two years before *Lembaga Melayu* wound up a new Malay daily made its appearance, the Singapore *Warta Malaya*, inaugurating a new and rather different era of newspaper journalism. This it will be more convenient to discuss systematically in a later section.

Returning to 1906, there appeared in Singapore in July of that year a monthly journal in Malay entitled *Al-Imam*, edited by Shaykh Mohd. Tahir Jalaluddin and later by Haji Abbas b. Mohd. Taha. This was the first Islamic reform journal to be published in Muslim South-east Asia, and consequently is still of considerable importance and interest. Modelled directly on the *Al-Manar* of reform circles in Cairo, *Al-Imam* was also the first in a long line of Malay periodicals devoted wholly or largely to religious (and most often to reform) matters, and the most influential of the group of four which appeared in the years 1906 to 1916. Two years after it stopped publication in early 1909, *Al-Imam* was succeeded by *Neracha*, also edited by Haji Abbas, which from 1911 to 1915 appeared every two weeks, then every ten days, and finally weekly. Nominally a newspaper, and indeed containing a fair proportion of straight news in its six folio-sized pages—principally news from the Middle East concerning the Italo-Turkish war, the Hejaz railway, and similar matters—*Neracha* has been grouped here with *Al-Imam* rather than with *Utusan Melayu* because at bottom its main concern was with religious persuasion and what is sometimes called 'pan-Islam'. It should, however, be said that it by no means ignored the local scene, and on socio-

[1] See below, pp. 19–22.

economic matters impinging on changes in traditional values—from the playing of football to the taking of bank interest—it propagated and discussed views which continue to be of interest to the social historian of urban Islam in Malaya and Singapore. The remaining two religious periodicals of this period need be mentioned only briefly. *Tunas Melayu*, a monthly brought out in association with *Neracha* and under the same editorship, ran from March 1913 for an unknown period (no copies now exist), and apparently has the distinction of having been the first Malay periodical to use photographic blocks for illustration. *Majallah al-Islam* (1914–15), propagating a more Ahmadiyya kind of reformism than its Al-Azhar influenced counterparts, consisted almost entirely of articles translated into Malay from the Woking (London) *Islamic Review* and was edited by the assistant editor of *Neracha* and *Tunas Melayu*, K. Anang. Some of the successors to these first Islamic periodicals in Malay will be discussed systematically in a later section.

The third phase

So much, then, for the first two phases (however arbitrarily determined) of the history of the Malay press, which had seen among other things the transition from lithography to movable type and from weekly to daily news journalism, and the rise of religious reform polemic. The remaining thirty-five years to 1941, which we may characterize as the third 'phase', saw the emergence of such a host of new titles and new types of publication that detailed discussion of all, or even a majority, becomes out of the question. It is possible, however, to make some generalizations about the major journalistic developments of the period, and about the principal sorts of publication that resulted. It is proposed to discuss the latter under some seven heads: daily and weekly newspapers, religious periodicals, periodicals published by teachers' associations and schools, literary periodicals, periodicals published by progress societies, and journals of entertainment. Throughout, except when historical interest determines otherwise, attention will be paid mainly to periodicals for which there are extant holdings.

Daily and weekly newspapers

Between 1930 and 1941 eight daily or 'near-daily' metropolitan newspapers were published in Malay, of which five were of particular influence, importance, and subsequent interest. The first and in some respects always the most powerful of these, *Warta Malaya*, has already been mentioned in passing. Started in January 1930 by members of the wealthy Alsagoff family in Singapore, it came to typify the ubiquity of Arab money in Malay journalism that was to characterize the 1930s. But if the 30s were the years of the hard-headed, Arab 'press barons', they were also the years during which a fully professional class of Malay journalists emerged, devoting their whole time and much of their lives to running newspapers, and the more senior of them— men like Othman Kalam, Onn b. Jaafar, Alwi al-Hadi, and Abdul Rahim

Kajai—moving regularly from one major editorial chair to another. Malay daily newspaper journalism up to 1930 had for twenty-three years, since the founding of *Utusan Melayu* in 1907, been tied to the English-language press and dominated by figures close to, and to this extent compromised by, the colonial government. With the founding of *Warta Malaya*, and finally with the demise of *Lembaga Melayu* in 1931, that era was gone for good and a new and tougher one begun. *Warta Malaya*'s editor for the first three years, Onn b. Jaafar, was an independent (if not yet independence) minded Malay of a new generation, and in the course of the depression years, with all their economic and political stresses, made the paper a forthright exponent of Malay views. It held this position under successive editors for the rest of the 1930s, ceasing publication only with the onset of the Japanese occupation.

Warta Malaya was joined in December 1931 by a second major paper which, though (like the third in this group) not technically a daily, was engaged in what was in essence daily journalism. *Majlis*, published in Kuala Lumpur twice weekly until the end of 1934 and then three times a week, and under the editorship for its first three years of the most brilliant of all Malay journalists, Abdul Rahim Kajai, profited from its position in the capital of the Federated Malay States to win wide readership among Malays throughout the peninsula and in the settlements. Like *Warta Malaya* it was partisan on behalf of a wide range of Malay causes, and played an especially important role (under the subsequent editorship of Othman Kalam) in the rise of the Malay state associations movement of the late 1930s. Contemporary with both *Warta Malaya* and *Majlis* in the early part of the decade, the third paper in this group, *Saudara* of Penang, had been founded as an Islamic reformist weekly paper in 1928 but started publishing twice weekly from 1932, shedding little of its reformism in the process but engaging much more fully in reportage and discussion of the political news of the day. Though an influential paper in many respects, and important for the general historian, *Saudara* became particularly noted for its creation, while under the editorship of Sayyid Alwi al-Hadi in 1934, of the Sahabat Pena literary society, the first Malay mass movement in the peninsula. Both *Saudara* and *Majlis* continued publication until the Japanese invasion, the latter subsequently being converted under Japanese auspices into a new paper entitled *Perubahan Bahru*, and resuming its old persona only after the war.

The fourth major daily of the 1930s was *Lembaga*, founded and edited by Onn b. Jaafar (with Singapore Arab financial support) in October 1935, following the earlier establishment of a weekly *Lembaga Malaya*. *Lembaga*, published first in Singapore and then, from 1938, in Johore Bahru, appears to have paid particular attention to Johore news and affairs, but adequate estimate of its strengths has been handicapped by the poverty of extant holdings, which though improved in recent years are worse than for any other major Malay daily of the period. The fifth and last paper of the group, the second *Utusan Melayu*, had a dramatic birth in 1939 which is recounted in

some detail in a reminiscent article by Yusoff Ishak in the anniversary publication *Utusan Melayu 10 Tahun*.[1] The product of strong feelings among
Singapore Malays concerning the need for a 'national organ' not dependent
on money from Arab or other alien sources, *Utusan Melayu* came into being
in May 1939 after a long share-pushing campaign among urban Malay taxi-
drivers and east coast padi farmers. Edited by Abdul Rahim Kajai, it appeared
daily until the Japanese occupation, always at the forefront of Malay nationalist
strivings (and in some commercial competition with *Warta Malaya* in particular), and is the only Malay newspaper (along with its stable companion
Utusan Zaman) to have survived continuously from before the war until the
present time.

Three remaining dailies, which did not acquire national status and were
in any case short lived, require brief mention. In February 1932 Mohd. Eunos
b. Abdullah, editor for seventeen years of the just defunct *Lembaga Melayu*,
tried to start a replacement on his own account, *Perkhabaran Dunia* of Penang.
It failed after only forty-five issues. A year later, also in Penang, another daily
was started, *Bumiputera*, under the editorship initially of Abdul Wahab b.
Abdullah, a recently returned graduate from Al-Azhar, and Othman Kalam.
Though it lasted for two years, and was a well-produced paper, its circulation
seems to have been confined largely to the north. Finally, the Ipoh *Warta
Kinta*, which had a brief life as a weekly from December 1937, and then failed,
resumed publication as a daily in September 1939, apparently with the
assistance of the English-language *Times of Malaya*. It ran throughout 1940,
but is not known after that date. Edited by Raja Mansor b. Raja Abdul Kadir,
a Sumatran Malay who had previously edited *Pewarta Deli* and *Deli Courant*
in Medan, and was also a well-known novelist, *Warta Kinta* contained some
first-class reporting of Malay affairs and is often a useful supplementary
source of information for the events of 1940.

Of the several news weeklies which, between 1916 and 1941, were of
particular interest and importance—and by news weeklies are meant those
periodicals which, appearing weekly (or occasionally more frequently), did
so primarily for the purpose of purveying news and comment rather than
entertainment, instruction, or some other commodity—perhaps some seven
or eight should be discussed briefly. *Idaran Zaman* (1925–30) was edited
in Penang by a Sumatran immigrant of Islamic reform interests who subsequently had an influential career in Malay journalism, Mohd. Yunus b.
Abdul Hamid, and later by Othman Kalam, who was to become one of the
'big four' among the journalists of the 1930s. *Lidah Benar* is of some interest
as the only periodical of any sort to publish in Klang, the royal capital and
second largest town of Selangor, though its reportage was not confined to that
area. Another Selangor paper to appear at about this time was the *Warta
Negeri* of Kuala Lumpur (1929–31), which prided itself on being 'the only
romanized Malay weekly paper in the Federated Malay States'. It came out

---

[1] *Utusan Melayu 10 Tahun* (Singapore, 1949), pp. 4–16.

twice weekly from May 1931 but seems to have failed shortly after. *Dewasa* (1931–2) and *Bahtera* (1932–3) were twice-weekly papers, one very much like the other, published in Penang and edited respectively by Mohd. Yunus b. Abdul Hamid and Othman Kalam, old colleagues and rivals in the past. Though unsuccessful in gaining a large enough audience to remain in publication they were workmanlike papers with good journalistic standards. In Kota Bharu, Kelantan, in 1934, a journal called *Al-Hikmah*, began publication (thrice-weekly at first, and then weekly from 1936), not in all senses a news magazine but containing much more information about east coast affairs than was generally available at the time, together with a selection of peninsular and foreign news and comment and some general articles. Edited by Ahmad b. Ismail (who had previously run a monthly called *Al-Hedayah*, also in Kota Bharu, and was a well-known translator and adaptor of Arabic fiction) *Al-Hikmah* rapidly became one of the more popular weeklies in circulation. *Lembaga Malaya* (1934–41), *Warta Ahad* (1935–41), and *Utusan Zaman* (1939–41) were Sunday issues or weekly news magazines published by the three major presses so named, in association with their respective dailies.

Religious periodicals

Periodicals wholly or largely concerned with the Islamic religion, whether from a prescriptive or some other point of view, constitute a frequent and important category of publication. Definition of what constitutes a religious periodical is not always easy at a time when homiletics, usually with an Islamic content, formed probably the most popular of Malay journalistic genres— few journals, even the more frivolous, did not devote some space to discussion of Islamic matters. Roughly speaking, however, there appear to have been between 1916 and 1941 some two dozen periodicals in Malay (and a further six in English) of a markedly Islamic kind, which divide easily into three groups convenient for discussion: general Islamic periodicals, those associated with educational institutions (mainly madrasah), and those associated with other sorts of religious organization (mainly clubs and societies). English-language periodicals will be discussed separately.

Mention has, of course, already been made of the earlier Islamic periodicals, *Al-Imam*, *Neracha*, and *Tunus Melayu*. The year 1917 saw the appearance of a new publication, emanating from the Majlis Ugama Islam in Kelantan, a semi-autonomous council set up under the authority of the sultan. *Pengasoh*, which appeared fortnightly until about 1932 and then weekly (and was also, it may be remarked, the first periodical of any consequence to be published outside the Straits Settlements) became in its own way one of the leading intellectual journals of the time, addressing itself to practical Islamic matters and related social and economic questions of contemporary concern. It circulated widely, if perhaps selectively, throughout Malaya. Not of assiduously reformist or other doctrinaire persuasion, it was contributed to by most of the leading Malay writers of the period with any sort of Islamic interest, and was often innovative in ideas. It is thought to have ceased publication at the end of 1937 (resuming after the war, and current today, if in rather different form), but unfortunately no holdings are known to exist for the period after 1927. In September 1926 there appeared in Penang a new monthly, *Al-Ikhwan*, under the editorship of Sayyid Shaykh b. Ahmad al-Hadi, a well-known religious reform writer and polemicist who had earlier been closely associated with *Al-Imam*. Though *Al-Ikhwan*, which came out regularly for a little over five years, was essentially an Islamic journal with a reformist purpose, it was also a social and even a political campaigner, and wrote in a lively and informed fashion about subjects as diverse as the emancipation of women and the provision of more English education for Malays, participating fully in all the controversies of the time and breaking lances with everybody from its fellow periodicals to the state religious authorities. Joined in 1928 by the weekly *Saudara* (already discussed as a newspaper of the 1930s) these two publications from Sayyid Shaykh's Jelutong Press played an important role in the vitalization of Malay society. An Islamic periodical of somewhat less influence but roughly equal circulation which appeared in 1929, also from Penang, and lasted for about eighteen months, was *Semangat Islam*, edited by Abdul Latif Hamidi. Espousing a fairly politicized kind of reformism, *Semangat Islam* was sometimes contributed to by Malay students at Al-Azhar in Cairo, and contained frequent articles about both the Middle East and Indonesia. It is in some ways reminiscent of the two Malay-language journals, *Seruan Azhar* (1925–8) and *Pilehan Timour* (1927–8), published by Malay and Indonesian students in Cairo, which circulated in the peninsula at this time.

Religious educational institutions in Malaya itself gave rise to a number of monthly periodicals, mostly short lived but of interest to the student of Islam and Islamic affairs in the peninsula. As none is especially distinctive, it is probably sufficient merely to list them, together with the madrasah or other school with which they were associated, and an occasional comment: *Al-Raja* (1925–6), Madrasah al-Mashhur, Penang; *Jasa* (1927–31), Madrasah al-Attas, Johore Bahru; *Temasek* (1930), Madrasah al-Juneid, Singapore (this journal seems to have been more ethnicist than Islamic in content); *Suara* (1931), Sharikat al-Ittihad al-Islamiah, Kota Bahru, Kelantan (this journal appeared weekly); *Panduan* (1934–5), Madrasah al-Idrisiah, Kuala Kangsar; *Bintang Malaya* (1939–41), Kuliah al-Firdaus, Singapore (the connection with the kuliah is unclear, and the journal may have been more general than Islamic); and *Seruan Ihya* (1941), Madrasah al-Ihya Abu Sharif, Gunong Semanggol, Perak.[1]

Of the periodicals known to have been associated with religious organizations of other sorts, five are worth particular mention. *Lidah Teruna* was

---

[1] A seventh journal, *Al-Hikmah* (1935), published by former students of the Madrasah al-Ma'arif al-Wataniah, Kepala Batas, Province Wellesley, of which no known holdings exist, may have been not a periodical proper but the publication in serial parts of a religious text or texts.

a fortnightly paper published between 1920 and 1921 by the Persekutuan
Perbahathan Orang2 Islam of Muar, in Johore, one of the first Malay voluntary associations of any kind to produce a magazine on its own account (the
first was the Persekutuan Keharapan Belia, in Johore Bahru, which had published *Harapan* the previous year). Then in 1926–7 the Persekutuan Guru2
Islam, Muar (which must surely have had many members in common with
the earlier debating society), brought out a monthly called *Lembaran Guru*.
In 1932, an organization calling itself the Pakatan Islam Johor (known
alternatively as Al-Jama'ah al-Islamiah al-Johoriah) brought out a single issue
(probably no more) of a rather slender magazine entitled *Al-Johoriah*, which
among other things lists in full the aims and objects of the society. An association of teachers in Islamic schools, which claimed to be peninsula-wide but
was centred on the Madrasah al-Mashhur in Penang, where it was known as
the Jama'ah Guru2 Ugama Semenanjong Melayu, began publishing a quarterly
there in 1935, entitled *Wihdatu'l-Madaris*. Although the extant holdings of
this periodical are very limited (and it is not known for how long it ran), it
appears to have been of some intellectual substance. Finally, in this group,
an organization in Penang calling itself the Pejabat al-Islam, but otherwise
obscure as to nature and purpose, began in July 1936 (and may thereupon also
have stopped) publishing a monthly called *Al-Islam*.

Six English-language periodicals devoted to Islamic matters are listed in the
Bibliography, either because Malays were in some way associated with their
production or because they are known to have circulated among the English-
educated. Only one, *The Modern Light*, was in all senses wholly Malay.
Founded and edited in Johore Bahru in May 1940 by Haji Abdul Majid b.
Zainuddin (previously Malayan Pilgrimage Officer and British Vice-Consul
in Jeddah) and his son Haji Abdul Latiph, *The Modern Light* described itself
as 'the only Malay national organ in English' and for eighteen monthly issues
published forthright and often polemical articles of a patriotic kind informed
by a lively Islamic spirit and some Islamic knowledge. The remaining five
English-language monthlies, all published in Singapore, can be listed only
briefly. *The Muslim* (1922–5), brought out by the Anjuman-i-Islam in conjunction with the Woking Muslim Mission, consisted (as had *Majallah al-
Islam*, in Malay, before it) of articles reprinted from the *Islamic Review*. It
almost certainly owed its launching to the visit to Malaya shortly before
of Kwaja Kamal-ud-Din, the principal figure associated with the Woking
Mission and an adherent of what was known as the Lahore branch of the
Ahmadiyya movement. *Real Islam* (1928–30), with at least one Malay on the
editorial board, espoused views that were markedly anti-Ahmadiyya. *Genuine
Islam* (1936–41) was the journal of the All-Malaya Muslim Missionary
Society, concerning the activities of which little is known by the present
writer. *The Muslim Messenger*, which appeared for a time in 1936, seems to
have been editorially Malay and was presumably missionary in intent. *Voice
of Islam* (1937–9), though nominally monthly, appeared rather irregularly and

like *Real Islam* was anti-Ahmadiyya in emphasis. Though Indian in inspiration, it appeared under the local patronage of Tengku Temenggong Ahmad of Johore.

Finally, mention should be made of two unclassifiable religious publications, if only to explicate their status, which was perhaps dubiously that of periodical. *Al-Kitab*, published in Kota Bharu (Kelantan) in 1920, was primarily a translation of the Kuran into Malay from Maulvi Muhammad Ali's version, with the addition of some general articles and stories, and an Arabic dictionary. Only four issues appeared. Similarly, *Puncha Pertikaian Ulama Islam*, published monthly in Penang in 1929–30, was a translation in serial parts of Averroes's *Bidayatu'l-Mujtahid Wa Nihayatu'l-Muktsaid.*

Periodicals published by (non-religious) teachers' associations or schools

School teachers, always among the better educated and more intellectually active of young Malays during these years, played an important role in all forms of journalism—as contributors, correspondents, critics, and of course purchasers and readers—but they also from time to time started periodicals of their own, one or two of which are among the more important of the period. The first journal sponsored by a teachers' association was a fairly small-scale affair, *Panduan Guru*, a monthly published by the Persekutuan Guru2 Melayu, Penang, which ran for three years from 1922. It was succeeded— superseded one might perhaps say—by what was to become one of the most influential Malay journals of opinion before the Second World War, the monthly *Majallah Guru*, published under the auspices of the combined Malay teachers' associations of Penang, Selangor, Negri Sembilan, and Malacca (joined later by those of Kelantan, Pahang, and Singapore). The two best-known editors of the journal were Mohd. b. Dato' Muda (1924–32), whose close interest in Malay journalism has contributed so largely to the historical record and to present holdings, and Mohd. Yasin b. Ma'mur (1933–8), who also had a substantial reputation as a poet. *Majallah Guru*, besides publishing educational articles of every conceivable sort, commented regularly on public affairs and nurtured a whole generation of Malay writers, being among other things the first periodical to publish original fiction, a development of some importance for the Malay short story.

Between 1930 and 1932 (and thereafter at rather spasmodic intervals) there appeared in Johore Bahru a magazine called *Bulan Melayu*, published by the Persekutuan Guru2 Perempuan Melayu, Johore, and distinguished as marking the first known foray of Malay women into journalism. *Bulan Melayu* was edited by Hajjah Zin bte Suleiman, who after the war was active in the women's section of UMNO and a leading parliamentarian. From 1940 *Bulan Melayu* appeared in conjunction with (though in separate format from) the quarterly *Idaman*, journal of the (male) Persekutuan Guru2 Melayu in Batu Pahat. In January 1936 the Persekutuan Guru2 Melayu, Singapore (which, it will be recalled, was already a participant in *Majallah Guru*), began to bring out an annual on its own account, *Saujana*, which continued to appear until at least 1940. And finally, among the teachers' association journals, the Persekutuan Guru2 Melayu, Perak, which had hitherto not been active in this field, started publishing in 1938 a periodical called *Semangat Guru*, which appeared three times a year for an unknown period.

Turning from the teachers' associations to colleges and schools (whose publications often involved teachers as well), there are five publications to note (concerning all of which, it must be said, holdings are lamentably poor). Two institutions in particular stand out in the history of Malay education in the early twentieth century—Malay College, Kuala Kangsar (which used to be styled 'the Eton of Malaya' and was predominantly for the sons of the well-born), and Sultan Idris Training College for teachers, at Tanjong Malim (which drew its students from the village level of society throughout the peninsula). Both the Malay College and Sultan Idris College produced periodicals. The first to appear, *Semaian*, was published at Malay College thrice-yearly from August 1923; unfortunately, in the absence of known holdings it is impossible to say for how long, and as the present writer has seen only one issue it is likewise impossible to characterize it. The same, alas, must be said of the college's second journal, known as *The Malay College Magazine*, which started publication annually in 1939. Shortly after *Semaian* first appeared, and perhaps prompted by a spirit of competition, Sultan Idris College began, in November 1923, to produce *Chendera Mata*, which came out twice yearly until shortly before the war. Present holdings are very deficient (and some have actually been lost since the 1961 listing) but it is clear that it was not merely a 'school magazine' (though in part this), but addressed itself to larger questions concerning Malay welfare, published articles by the teaching staff, and original fiction and poetry. In view of Sultan Idris Training College's important role as the focus of what may be termed the Malay cultural revival, the journal remains of interest and importance. A fourth school publication (of which, again, little or nothing is known owing to absence of holdings) was the monthly journal in English, *The Torch*, produced in 1928 by former pupils of the Majlis Ugama English School in Kota Bharu, Kelantan. Finally, in 1934, a quarterly journal appeared in Penang in connection with the Chowrasta Malay School, by 1936 being published under the auspices of 'the Malay schools of Penang and Seberang Prai'. Though in no sense an official journal, it was run by Malay teachers, school inspectors, and education department officials, and contained news of the schools and their activities and some contributions by pupils, as well as more general articles.

Literary periodicals

Modern Malay literature—whether in the shape of adaptations from other languages, original short stories, poems, serial novels, drolleries, topical sketches, or other literary forms—is inextricably linked with the expansion of

Malay journalism in the 1920s and 30s. *Majallah Guru* (and later other monthlies as well), the weeklies of the decade before the war—*Warta Ahad, Warta Jenaka, Lembaga Malaya, Utusan Zaman* and others—all regularly published short stories and similar material. The writers—men like Abdul Rahim Kajai, Ishak b. Haji Muhammad, Muhammad Yasin b. Ma'mur and others—became household names. To suggest a special category of 'literary periodical' may therefore seem superfluous, perhaps even misleading. On the other hand, there were a number of journals which existed *only* for or in association with literary purposes, and it seems worth making clear which these were.

The first journal, it would appear, to devote itself entirely to the publication of fiction—recognizing, perhaps, the new market coming into existence for writing in this genre—was *Chahaya Bintang*, a little monthly published in Seremban briefly in 1926–7. Most of the other purely short-story magazines came later, at the end of the 1930s, but in the interim there appeared a series of journals associated with literary societies which it is useful to consider together. *Taja Penghiboran* (1934–5) was published quarterly by the literary section of the (Malay) Muar Club in Johore and devoted mainly to the writings of its members. During these same years the organization Sahabat Pena, started in Penang, was building its peninsula-wide influence through the medium of the newspaper *Saudara*. In 1938, at the peak of its success (with a membership of some 12,000) the club headquarters in Penang started a monthly journal *Paspam* (otherwise known as *Pemberita Pejabat Persaudaraan Sahabat Pena Malaya*, or *Pemberita Pejabat Paspam*) containing news, views, and original writing, which circulated to members and others interested. The editor, and the man who must be credited with the idea that had given birth to this friends-of-the-pen club, was Mohd. Arifin Ishak. Later, in 1940, Arifin also edited the club's annual, *Taman Paspam*, which was able to appear only once before the outbreak of war. Two other publications associated with Sahabat Pena were *Suara Pena*, a monthly published by the Singapore branch for five months from September 1938, succeeded in January 1939 by *Pancharan Pena*, produced by the younger members of the same branch, which came out fortnightly for an uncertain but probably brief period.

Returning to literary magazines proper—though perhaps not in all cases to profound literary art—a group of five came out in fairly rapid succession in the years immediately before the war. *Majallah al-Riwayat*, published fortnightly (later monthly) in Kota Bharu, Kelantan, in 1938–9, and edited by Ishak b. Lutfi Omar, who later became state Mentri Besar, began by concentrating entirely on short stories, later including other types of material as well. *Majallah Cherita*, published monthly in Penang in 1938–9, dealt only in short stories, many of a romantic kind—as presumably did two other magazines published in 1941, of which little trace beyond their titles now remains: *Majallah Romans*, of Singapore, and *Belenggu Perkasehan*, of Ipoh. Much more important in artistic terms—and a journal which continued to be influential after the war—was the last of the literary group, *Mastika*, published monthly in 1941 in conjunction with the Utusan papers and edited by Abdul Rahim Kajai.

Periodicals published by progress associations

It will be clear that among those periodicals already described were many which were the offspring of clubs and societies of some kind—whether religious in impulse, educational, or literary. There are, however, a number of other publications which are not so easily classified, and yet which found their origin in that highly characteristic activity of the 1920s and 30s, the forming of voluntary associations for a great variety of different ends broadly related to the circumstances of the modern world, its needs and demands. Many of these unclassifiable groups, not linked to specific occupational or intellectual interests, may perhaps be called 'progress associations', for all usually had in common the aim of improving the prospects of their members and of the wider community to which they belonged. Progress associations of this energetic but rather unfocused kind seem to have been particularly characteristic of the 1920s (the 1930s, one might suggest, sharpened for many Malays the issues on which common action was necessary), and it is during these years that societies of this kind, as an important part of their activities, often published a journal.

The first of these (and its title, as with many others, is indicative of its nature) was *Harapan*, published irregularly in Johore Bahru in 1919 and 1920 by an association calling itself the Persekutuan Keharapan Belia. A few years later, in Seremban, a quarterly entitled *Tetauan Muda* was published in 1923–7 by the Persekutuan Rembau Ternakkan—as befitted Negri Sembilan, perhaps a rather localized variant of the progress association. *Masa*, journal of the Persekutuan Suloh Pelajaran in Muar, appeared more or less monthly (it has a very confused bibliographical history) from 1927–8, and was revived for a time in 1934. In Singapore, a group calling itself the Sharikat Suloh-Menyuloh produced a fortnightly paper, *Penyuloh*, during 1924 and 1925. *Perjumpaan Melayu*, published briefly in Muar in 1925, and its successor the longer lived *Panji2 Melayu* (1925–9), were published by an association calling itself the Maharani Company, empowered by its by-laws to open a trading concern, buy a rubber plantation, run a madrasah, or start a newspaper—though only the last is known to have eventuated. In 1925, the Malay Literary Society in Kuala Lumpur changed its name to become the Persekutuan Kemajuan Pengetahuan, and broadened its activities to include, among other things, publication of a quarterly journal *Kemajuan Pengetahuan* (which appeared for only two issues). In Pasir Puteh, Kelantan, in 1927, an association called the Persekutuan New Club published a monthly journal (for an unknown period) entitled *Terok*. And even in Kuching, the only Malay periodical known to have been published in Sarawak before the war, *Fajar Sarawak* (1930), was brought out by a group of young Malays organized in a Sharikat Putera Sarawak. Publications of the kind detailed above were seldom concerned to record the affairs of their parent associations—their purpose, rather, was to provide informative and educative reading matter for the members and for Malays at large, and to allow the members to stretch their intellectual muscle by writing about affairs of the day.

Journals of entertainment

Until the late 1920s most Malay periodicals were largely didactic in purpose. Even the newspapers, some of which came nearest to providing a little light relief from time to time, were primarily serious in intent. And there could be no question about the earnestness of the religious periodicals, the teachers' journals, the progress association monthlies, and the like. The fact was that to a considerable degree literate Malay society at this time was largely engaged in educating itself, in the tasks of self-strengthening, in drawing the moral from events, and in seizing and improving the moment. There was little time for literary frivolity and in the absence of a mass audience or much of a leisure class little taste for it. With changes in demography and literacy, however—with more people living in towns, able to read, having time and a little money to spare and electric light to see by—there arose an audience which asked to be entertained, not just improved.

The first indications of this, perhaps, came with a rise in the entertainment content of otherwise sober journals—the publication of the 'Rokambul' detective stories in *Al-Ikhwan* by that astute journalist Sayyid Shaykh al-Hadi is a good case in point. Short stories and serial novels began to appear more frequently in the ordinary press, humorous sketches and up-to-date versions of the traditional Pa' Pandir tales, riddle and joke columns, episodes of the *Thousand and One Nights*, and light-weight 'popular knowledge' articles on anything from the art of the conjuror to the history of ballooning. Before long, however, there began to emerge as a distinct genre the periodical which set out solely to amuse, relax, and entertain—in short, to provide 'a good read'. There are many examples, but it may suffice to cite the six or seven magazines published and edited in Singapore between 1932 and about 1937 by Suleiman b. Ahmad, the single most determined purveyor of light reading in the 1930s—apart, that is, from the big Warta and Lembaga presses, which did so as a by-product of other activities. Suleiman was not completely without the desire to instruct his fellows (even if only to be fashionable), as his first papers, the monthlies *Kemajuan Melayu* and *Tanah Melayu*, reveal, but when these found themselves banned by the religious authorities of certain states, for alleged salacity, he devoted himself increasingly to unashamed entertainment, publishing in succession *Dunia Sekarang*, *Shorga Dunia*, *Melayu Muda*, *Penggeli Hati*, and possibly others. Suleiman may not have been wholly representative of the genre but he was certainly the most enthusiastic of his kind (and *Tanah Melayu* in its first year appears to have sold more copies per issue than any previous Malay periodical), and it may perhaps be argued that, in admass terms, Malay journalism finally came of age with the regular appearance of magazines devoted to entertainment, a process consummated in 1941 with the appearance of the first *Film Melayu*, inevitable sign and symbol of a flourishing pop culture of a modern kind.

Summary

In the preceding account, as will be evident, a large number of periodicals have gone without mention. It must not be supposed that those passed over were without contemporary (or have no present) interest or importance. Some are omitted because they have not been used by the compiler in his own research (either because there are no known holdings or for other reasons) and many of the remainder because of the sheer impossibility of getting everything in. Additional categories of analytical interest could perhaps have been developed—women's periodicals, for instance, or regional publications. Why did so many periodicals originate in Muar, Johore? What was their general character, and what relationship did they bear to the Malay society of the time? Is it relevant that Muar rather than Johore Bahru, the state capital, has been the focus of Malay political energies in the period since the war? The same sorts of question might be raised in a more general way of Kota Bharu in Kelantan; and their obverse of Pahang which, despite giving birth to several notable Malay intellectuals in the 1920s and 30s, produced not a single paper. In the absence of systematic discussion of all periodicals by region, which might have prompted other questions of this sort, an index of titles arranged by state of origin has been provided at the back of the *Bibliography*.

To turn to another matter, Malay journalism, it is clear, is absolutely central to the development of modern forms of the language and to modern Malay literature. Though no attempt has been made here to explore issues of this sort, several studies of these and related matters have been made by others, most of which will be found listed in the bibliography at the rear.

The remaining topic of substance, then, apart from some remarks concerning the holdings themselves, is who did the periodicals reach, and who read them?

Circulation and readership

Questions concerning circulation, though obviously of importance in some respects, are extremely difficult to answer satisfactorily. To start with, no information at all (except of an occasional and incidental kind) is available for periodicals published in the peninsular states. Even for the Straits Settlements, the figures appearing annually in the statistical *Blue Books* published by the government ignore many periodicals and give incomplete information concerning others. Though it may perhaps be assumed that the official figures represent the average total number of copies sold per issue, it is not in fact known whether the sales were those taking place solely in the Straits Settlements (thus excluding sales in either the peninsula or the Netherlands Indies,

or both), nor whether a true statistical average was taken or merely a hypothetical figure provided by the publisher and based on numbers printed (as
certain evidence suggests). Further problems arise because single-issue figures
of this kind cannot in any way reflect fluctuations within the year—something
of particular relevance for first and last years of publication, and for periodicals
either published for periods shorter than a calendar year, or beginning and
ending in or near mid-year.

At best, then, the *Blue Book* statistics can provide only a very approximate
and incomplete guide to Malay periodical circulation, and should be interpreted with the greatest caution. Nor should it be forgotten that sales or
circulation figures alone, however accurate, are an insufficient index of the
penetration of printed matter in peasant societies undergoing modernization.
An institution such as the coffee shop often ensures that one copy of a daily
or weekly paper is read anything from a dozen to a hundred times. And even
where illiteracy is common, as one writer observed of the Malay states in
1940, 'Often, of an evening, one [may see] at the wayside Chinese shop some
lettered man, perhaps an old *guru* of the local school or perhaps the local
penghulu, reading one or other of these papers, and a little crowd of elderly
people less literate than he eagerly listening, questioning, and commenting
around him'.[1]

Subject to all these qualifications, then, the four tables that follow give the
circulation or sale per issue of those periodicals listed in the Straits Settlements *Blue Book* from 1877 to 1938, the first and last years for which statistics
were published. Table I covers the years from 1877 to 1900 (omitting those
for which no Malay periodicals were recorded). Table II covers the years
from 1901 to 1919. Tables III and IV cover the years from 1920 to 1938,
Table III listing the more important periodicals (and especially the dailies
and news weeklies), and Table IV the less important. For the sake of quick
comparison, the frequency of publication of each periodical is indicated by
the small letter above the first entry, additional letters over subsequent
entries indicating a change in frequency. The letters are to be interpreted
as follows: d = daily, 3xw = thrice-weekly, 2xw = twice-weekly, w =
weekly, f = fortnightly, and m = monthly. The letter 't' is placed above
those entries for which the *Blue Books* give only the total for the year.

A note on holdings

The most important change to record in the position described in 1961 is that
the University of Malaya Library has transferred all its holdings of pre-1941
periodicals to the Arkib Negara Malaysia (National Archives of Malaysia) in
Kuala Lumpur, for preservation and safe keeping. The decision to do this cannot but be welcomed by those interested in safeguarding the Malay journalistic

---

[1] Zainal Abidin b. Ahmad, 'Malay Journalism in Malaya', *Journal of the Royal Asiatic
Society, Malayan Branch*, XIX, 2 (1941), p. 249. The substance of this paper had previously
been delivered as a Rotary Club talk in March 1940.

TABLE I

	1877	1878	1879	1880	1881	1882	1883	1884	1885	1886	1887	1888	1889	1890	1891	1892	1893	1894
Jawi Peranakan	(w) 200	200	250	250	250	250	250	250	165	300	300	250	85	250	250	275	250	185
Shamsu'l-Kamar		(w) 150																
Sekola Melayu												(w) 250	200	250				
Bintang Timor																		(d) 200

TABLE II

	1901	1902	1903	1904	1905	1906	1907	1908	1909	1910	1911	1912	1913	1914	1915	1916	1917	1918	1919
Chahaya Pulau Pinang	(w) 600	600	600	600	500	450	450												
Taman Pengetahuan				(w) 500	500	400 (m)	500												
Al-Imam						2,000	1,500 (3xw)												
Utusan Melayu							600	600 (w)	600	600	1,050	1,150	1,100	1,200	1,200	1,200 (d)	1,100	1,100	1,100
Chahaya Matahari								500											
Al-Watan									(f) 1,000	1,000 (w)									
Malaysia Advocate										200	345 (f)	(w) 600							
Neracha											700	600	700	500 (m)					
Majallah al-Islam														200					
Lembaga Melayu														(d) 900	450	600	400	400	800

TABLE III

	1920	1921	1922	1923	1924	1925	1926	1927	1928	1929	1930	1931	1932	1933	1934	1935	1936	1937	1938
Lembaga Melayu	(d) 1,000	1,000	1,200	1,200	1,200 (w)	1,200	1,200	1,300	1,400	1,400	1,400	800							
Idaran Zaman					700	1,200	1,300 (w) 1,000 (m)	1,500	1,100	1,500	1,500								
Suara Malaya							1,000	1,000											
Al-Ikhwan							1,000	1,000	1,000 (w)	750	700	500							
Saudara									1,000	1,500	1,400 (d)	1,500	(2xw) 1,000	1,800	1,500	1,500	1,500	1,100	1,000
Warta Malaya											1,000	1,500	2,000	2,000	2,500	3,000	2,500	2,700	2,750
Chahaya Timor										(w) 1,000									
Dewasa												(2xw) 2,000							
Bahtera												(2xw) 1,000	2,000 (2xw)						
Suara Benar													550						
Lembaga Malaya																(w) 2,400	2,300		
Warta Ahad																(w) 3,000	3,000	4,000	4,000
Lembaga																(d) 850	(w) 800		
Warta Jenaka																	2,400	3,850	4,000

Table IV

	1923	1924	1925	1926	1927	1928	1929	1930	1931	1932	1933	1934	1935	1936	1937	1938
The Muslim	(m) 400	(t) 2,800	2,800	1,500	700	700										
Kabar Kawat Melayu		(w) 500	(t) 6,000													
Kabar Uchapan Baru				(w) 500	500	500	500	500								
Perdagangan						(m) 1,000				(t) 1,700	(m) 200					
Real Islam							(m) 1,000									
Semangat Islam								1,700								
Bintang Pranakan								(w) 1,500								
Kanak-Kanak									(t) 2,500							
Tanah Melayu												(m) 3,500	2,000	1,500	(t) 10,000	
Dunia Sekarang												(f) 2,500	1,500			
Chahaya Singapura												(m) 1,000	1,000			
The Story Teller													(f) 1,000			
Medan Laki-Laki													(w) 1,000			
Kahidupan Dunia Akhirat													(f) 1,500			
Dunia Akhirat													4,000	(m) 1,500	2,500	

past—and by the shade of the late Muhammad b. Dato' Muda, whose laboriously gathered private collection formed a large part of the University's important holdings. The Arkib Negara, which has been able to make many acquisitions of its own in recent years, has an extremely efficient repair and maintenance division which has already laminated many thousand sheets of old newsprint, and it continues to salvage those parts of its holdings which are in need of restoration.

As a result of these combined operations, the Arkib Negara Malaysia is now the repository of incomparably the best collection of Malay periodicals in existence—a collection which, it must be hoped, it will be allowed to look after for many years to come. In the course of the transfer of the University's periodicals, all items have been microfilmed either by the Arkib Negara or by the University itself, and details will be found in the *Bibliography*. The University of Singapore continues to hold negative microfilm of a large number of the papers comprising the original University of Malaya collection.

The Dewan Bahasa dan Pustaka in Kuala Lumpur, mainly as a result of acquisitions made in recent years, possesses runs of a number of periodicals of importance, many of which are not found elsewhere, and it is unfortunate that the Library of the Dewan has had such great difficulty in looking after them properly. The fact that the Dewan is responsible for a great variety of important tasks of more immediate practical relevance is no doubt a principal reason why the card catalogue of Malay periodicals is badly organized and incomplete, and the periodicals themselves scattered in different parts of the Dewan, often rather badly housed. Many, unhappily, are in poor condition and deteriorating, and it is to be hoped that before long circumstances will permit arrangements to be made to remedy this. The ideal solution would undoubtedly be for the Dewan to do as the University has, and transfer its holdings of pre-1941 periodicals to the Arkib Negara for safe keeping. Were this to be done, the Arkib would become trustee of a unified collection of national-language periodicals of a kind not paralleled elsewhere in Southeast Asia.

The other repository of major importance, included for the first time in the present bibliography, is the British Museum Library in London. The Museum's collection is an excellent and coherent one, supplementing the Malaysian holdings in several respects, and it is to be hoped that portions of it can in due course be microfilmed. With one exception (the *Straits Chinese Herald*), the Museum holdings are housed in the Great Russell Street premises, not at Colindale, and access may be obtained through the Oriental Printed Books and Manuscripts Department of the Library.

The National Library of Singapore continues to hold a small quantity of Malay periodicals, some of which supplement other known holdings. Improvements in the organization of the Library since its removal into new premises from the old Raffles Museum building have made it easier to verify holdings and obtain access.

Of the four private individuals listed in 1961 as repositories, one, Tuan Haji Hamdan b. Shaykh Tahir, subsequently gave his holdings to the University of Malaya Library, where they were amalgamated with the existing holdings and have now been transferred to the Arkib Negara. Although Dato' Haji Ahmad b. Ismail, of Kota Bharu, died in 1969, his holdings remain in the possession of his family. It is hoped that, as with those of Tan Sri Haji Zainal Abidin b. Ahmad and Tuan Haji Mohd. Zain b. Ayob, they will in due course come into the possession of the nation.

To sum up, in the decade and more which has elapsed since the *Guide to Malay Periodicals* first appeared, known holdings have been greatly added to, further loss and physical deterioration has on the whole been halted, and microfilming has increased. Although of the 173 periodicals enumerated in the basic list 37 are not represented in any collection (compared with 45 out of the comparable list of 144 in 1961), it must be said that many of these are known to have been slight and ephemeral. In the same way, though by no means all the existing holdings are of complete runs, few periodicals of long duration or known importance are now seriously deficient. Finally, the regularity with which in the past ten years small collections of periodicals have continued to turn up in out-of-the-way places offers reasonable promise that holdings will for some time continue to grow.

Organization of the bibliography

The bibliography is divided into three sections. The first and much the largest lists the 173 periodicals known to have been published in the Malay language or under Malay auspices in the states now comprising Malaysia and Singapore between 1876 and 1941. The vast majority of these are entirely in Malay, and overwhelmingly in the Jawi script, but a few are wholly or partly in English.

The second section lists the fifteen periodicals known to have been published in Arabic in Singapore during this period, and therefore of particular interest to students of Islam in the region.

The third section lists nine periodicals known to have been published in the Malay language, but under Christian mission auspices, during the period from 1852 (the date of the first) to 1941.

WILLIAM R. ROFF

New York

FORM OF ENTRY

THE form of entry is straightforward. Listing is in strict chronological order, by date of the first issue. On the first line, in capital letters, is the name of the periodical. Transliteration of Jawi names is idiosyncratic: where the periodical itself has provided a Rumi version of the name, I have usually adhered to this; where it has not, I have tried to use the contemporaneously accepted version.

The second line gives the place of origin, followed by the frequency, followed by the dates of publication. It will be noticed that while in almost all cases the date of the first issue is known, the date of the last very often is not. Where a reasonably probable terminal date is available, I have given this with a query. Although many of the periodicals were dated according to the Muslim calendar, I have thought it best to give all dates in the Western style.

The third line gives, where possible, the name or names of the editors. Here again problems arise in transliterating from the Jawi. One can do no more than give the Rumi usage of the person concerned, where this is known, and in other cases give the most common spelling of the name in peninsular Malaya. Except in some special instances, variations on the name Muhammad are represented as 'Mohd.'

On the fourth and subsequent lines are listed the known holdings in Malaysia and the United Kingdom. The abbreviations used to indicate location are given below.

Finally, there are brief notes on particular points of interest.

Unless otherwise stated, all periodicals are printed in the Jawi (modified Arabic) script.

ABBREVIATIONS

AN   Arkib Negara Malaysia (National Archives of Malaysia), Kuala Lumpur

BM   British Museum Library, London

DB   Dewan Bahasa dan Pustaka (Language and Literature Agency), Kuala Lumpur

NL   National Library, Singapore

UM   University of Malaya Library, Kuala Lumpur

US   University of Singapore Library, Singapore

Ahmad   Dato' Haji Ahmad b. Ismail, Kota Bharu, Kelantan

Zaba   Tan Sri Haji Zainal Abidin b. Ahmad, Kuala Lumpur

Zain   Haji Muhammad Zain b. Ayob, Pasir Puteh Bharu, Perak

In the case of the six institutions only, possession of physical originals is indicated by an asterisk, *. Holdings on microfilm are indicated by ° for negative film, and by † for positive film. The holdings of the three individuals are of originals.

GMP   William R. Roff, *Guide to Malay Periodicals, 1876–1941* (Singapore, 1961)

TSK   Muhammad b. Dato' Muda, *Tarikh Surat Khabar* (Bukit Mertajam, 1940).

SECTION ONE: MALAY

1. JAWI PERANAKAN
Singapore; weekly; 1876–[April 1895]
Editors: Munshi Mohd. Said b. Dada
Mohyiddin, 1876–88; Munshi Mohd.
Ali b. Ghulam al-Hindi, 1888–[?]
Holdings:
AN*, US°, UM°: Vol. XI, Nos. 511–46
(Jan.–Sept. 1887); XII, Nos. 547–611
(Sept. 1887–Dec. 1888); XIII, Nos.
612–62 (Jan.–Dec. 1889); XIV, Nos.
663–709 (Jan.–Dec. 1890); XV, Nos.
710–60 (Jan.–Dec. 1891); XVI, Nos.
761–810 (Jan.–Dec. 1892); XVII,
Nos. 811–77 (Jan. 1893–July 1894);
XVIII, Nos. 878–915 (July 1894–
Apr. 1895)
BM*: Vol. V, Nos. 214, 217–18, 224–5,
248 (Mar., Apr., June 1881)

[Note: This, the first Malay-language
newspaper in either Malaysia or Indonesia,
was also the longest-lived in Malaysia
before 1941. The first editor, Mohd. Said,
was of Indian Muslim extraction, born in
Penang, and, in addition to managing the
paper until his death in 1888, taught at
Raffles Institution in Singapore.]

2. NUJUMU'L-FAJAR
Singapore; weekly; 4 September 1877–
[187?]
Editor:
Holdings:

[Note: This hand-lithographed paper was
also called *Idaran Bintang Timor* (according to *TSK*, p. 99), and may have been the
same as that referred to by E. W. Birch
('The Vernacular Press in the Straits',
p. 51) as *Bintang Barat*. If the latter, it
had ceased publication by January 1880.]

3. SHAMSU'L-KAMAR
Singapore; weekly; [187?–187?]
Editor:
Holdings:

[Note: Although the dates are unknown,
this paper seems to have been concurrent

for some time with *Nujumu'l-Fajar*, and
had ceased publication by January 1880.
E. W. Birch ('The Vernacular Press in the
Straits', p. 51) gives the title as *Peridaran
Shamsu Walkamer*, and by analogy with
the known alternative title for *Nujumu'l-
Fajar* it may indeed have been called
Idaran Shamsu'l-Kamar. It was almost
certainly hand-lithographed.]

4. SEKOLA MELAYU
Singapore; weekly; 1 August 1888–[?]
Editor: Munshi Mohd. Ali b. Ghulam
al-Hindi
Holdings:
AN*, US°, UM°: Vol. I, Nos. 1–21, 23–
50 (Aug. 1888–July 1889); II, Nos.
53–62, 64–7, 69–76, 81–4, 90 (Aug.
1890–[? Dec. 1890])

[Note: The spelling 'Sekola' is as given.
The paper was hand-lithographed. Volume
II was erratic in appearance, with un-
explained breaks in time between Nos. 62
and 64 and Nos. 76 and 81, in particular.
The face date of the last extant issue is as
given, but does not fit the series. Lim,
*Newspapers Published in the Malaysian
Area*, p. 177, lists an additional positive
microfilm of this paper held by the library
of Nanyang University, Singapore.]

5. STRAITS CHINESE HERALD
Singapore; daily; 22 January 1891–[?]
(Rumi, and partly English)
Editor:
Holdings:
BM*: Vol. I, Nos. 1–87 (Jan.–May 1891)

[Note: Alternatively entitled *Surat Khabar
Peranakan*, this paper was produced by
Straits Chinese and contained news and
editorials in English, with a varying
amount translated into Malay. It was the
first Malay-language periodical to publish
in the roman script.]

6. SERI PERAK
   Taiping; weekly; June 1893–[?]
   Editor: [? Haji Abdul Kadir b. Setia Raja]
   Holdings:

   [Note: The first newspaper in any language
   to be published in the Protected Malay
   States, this appears to have been associated
   with Sayyid Abdul Hassan b. Burhan,
   founder of the bi-weekly English-language
   Perak Pioneer, which began publication in
   July 1894. See, e.g., W. Makepeace, 'The
   Press', in A. Wright and H. A. Cartwright
   (eds.), *Twentieth Century Impressions of
   British Malaya*; and cf. also *Jajahan
   Melayu*, below.]

7. BINTANG TIMOR
   Singapore; daily to March 1895, thrice-
   weekly thereafter; 2 July 1894–2 July
   1895 (Rumi)
   Editor: Song Ong Siang
   Holdings:
       AN*°, US°, UM+: Vol. I, Nos. 1–154
       (July–Dec. 1894); II, Nos. 1–112
       (Jan.–July 1895)
       BM*: Vol. I, Nos. 1–154; II, Nos.
       1–112

   [Note: The first wholly Malay-language
   daily newspaper in Malaysia or Singapore,
   this was published by the Chinese Christian
   Association but was not in any way concerned to proselytize.]

8. TANJONG PENEGERI
   Penang; twice-weekly; 4 October 1894–[?]
   Editor: S. P. S. K. Kadar Sahib
   Holdings:
       BM*: Vol. I, Nos. 1–43 (Oct. 1894–
       Mar. 1895)

   [Note: The name appears to derive from
   an old name for Georgetown, in Penang,
   Tanjong Penaga (*TSK*, p. 102). The paper
   was hand-lithographed.]

9. PEMIMPIN WARTA
   Penang; weekly; 4 November 1895–[?]
   Editor:
   Holdings:
       BM*: Vol. I, Nos. 1–33 (Nov. 1895–
       June 1896); II, Nos. 34–84 (June
       1896–July 1897)

   [Note: The transliteration of the title on
   the masthead of this hand-lithographed
   paper is 'Warita', and it is entered under
   this in the British Museum catalogue.]

10. JAJAHAN MELAYU
    Taiping; weekly; 5 November 1896–
    [? month] 1897
    Editors: Mohd. Omar b. Haji Bakar (to
    3 July 1897); Ghulam Kadar (10 July–
    26 Aug. 1897); Sayyid Abdul Hassan
    b. Burhan (26 Aug.–21 Oct. 1897)
    Holdings:
        AN*: Vol. I, Nos. 1–9 (Nov.–Dec.
        1896); II, Nos. 10–42 (Jan.–Oct.
        1897)
        BM*: Vol. I, Nos. 1–9; II, Nos. 10–42

    [Note: A hand-lithographed paper pub-
    lished by Sayyid Abdul Hassan b. Burhan
    under the auspices of the English-
    language weekly *The Perak Pioneer*; cf.
    also *Seri Perak*, above.]

11. WARTA KERAJAAN PERAK
    Taiping; monthly to 1904, thereafter
    twice-monthly; January 1897–[? 1910]
    (Jawi to April 1905, Rumi thereafter)
    Editor:
    Holdings:
        BM*: Vol. I, Nos. 1–12 (Jan.–Dec.
        1897); II, Nos. 1–12 (Jan.–Dec.
        1898); III, Nos. 1–16 (Jan.–Nov.
        1899); IV, Nos. 1–12 (Jan.–Dec.
        1900); V, Nos. 1–14 (Jan.–Dec.
        1901); VI, Nos. 1–13 (Jan.–Dec.
        1902); VII, Nos. 1–14 (Jan.–Dec.
        1903); VIII, Nos. 1–12 (Jan.–Dec.
        1904); IX, Nos. 1–21 (Jan.–Dec.
        1905); X, Nos. 1–27 (Jan.–Dec.
        1906); XI, Nos. 1–26 (Jan.–Dec.
        1907); XII, Nos. 1–26 (Jan.–Dec.
        1908); XIII, Nos. 1–26 (Jan.–Dec.
        1909); XIV, No. 2 (Jan. 1910)
        AN*: Vol. XII, Nos. 1–26; XIV, No. 1

    [Note: A Malay edition of the *Perak
    Government Gazette*. The *Gazette* itself
    ceased publication at the end of 1909.]

12. LENGKONGAN BULAN

Penang; weekly; 30 April 1900–[?]
Editor: Mohd. Ali b. Harun al-Hindi
Holdings:
> AN*, US°, UM°: Vol. I, Nos. 3–5, 9,
> 12–14, 23–8 (May–Nov. 1900)
> BM*: Vol. I, Nos. 1–44/45 (Apr. 1900–
> Mar. 1901)

[Note: A hand-lithographed paper.]

13. BINTANG TIMOR

Penang; weekly; 1 March–[September]
1900
Editor: Abdul Ghani b. Mohd. Kassim
Holdings:
> AN*°, UM+, US°: Vol. I, Nos. 1–23,
> 25–8, 30 (Mar.–Sept. 1900)
> BM*: Vol. I, Nos. 1–23, 25–8, 30

[Note: This was succeeded, for reasons unknown, by *Chahaya Pulau Pinang* in October 1900, under the same editorship. Not to be confused with the Singapore *Bintang Timor*, first published in July 1894. The BM holdings contain a note, 'Nos. 24 and 29 not procurable on account of failure of the press', and it may be observed that these issues are missing from the other known holding.]

14. CHAHAYA PULAU PINANG

Penang; weekly; 13 October 1900–
[? March 1908]
Editor: Abdul Ghani b. Mohd. Kassim
Holdings:
> BM*: Vol. I, Nos. 1–52 (Oct. 1900–
> Oct. 1901); II, Nos. 1–52 (Oct.
> 1901–Oct. 1902); III, Nos. 1–52
> (Oct. 1902–Oct. 1903); IV, Nos. 2–
> 52 (Oct. 1903–Oct. 1904); V, Nos.
> 1–52 (Oct. 1904–Sept. 1905); VI,
> Nos. 1–53 (Oct. 1905–Oct. 1906);
> VII, Nos. 1–19, 21–52 (Oct. 1906–
> Oct. 1907); VIII, Nos. 1–25 (Oct.
> 1907–Mar. 1908)
> AN*°, UM+, US°: Vol. IV, Nos. 13,
> 15–17, 19–22, 24–52; V, Nos. 1–12;
> VI, Nos. 15–16, 19–20, 22–5, 28–9,
> 32–4, 39–40, 43

[Note: According to *TSK* (p. 121), this paper was produced under the (Chinese) auspices of the owners of the Criterion Press.]

15. JAMBANGAN WARTA

Batu Gajah; weekly; May 1901–[?]
Editor:
Holdings:

[Note: A hand-lithographed paper.]

16. TAMAN PENGETAHUAN

Singapore; weekly; 1 June 1904–[?]
Editors: Munshi Mohd. Ali b. Ghulam al-Hindi; Sayyid Mahmud b. Abdul Kadir al-Hindi
Holdings:

[Note: This paper was owned by Alwi Brothers of Singapore, and printed by Alwi b. Abdul Kadir al-Hindi. The principal editor had previously edited *Jawi Peranakan*, until its demise in 1895. His nephew Sayyid Mahmud, besides being a linguist of note, was the author of numerous school textbooks in Malay, prepared for the Education Department. The issue of the paper appearing on 1 June 1904 was actually a 'sample' issue (*perchontohan*), the first regular issue appearing on 6 June.]

17. KHIZANAH AL-ILMU

Kuala Kangsar; monthly; August 1904–
[?]
Editor: Sayyid Abdullah al-Attas
Holdings:

[Note: Others involved in the production of this hand-lithographed paper were Raja Osman b. Raja Ja'afar (*kepala atas pekerjaan*), Haji Mohd. Noor b. Haji Mohd. Ismail al-Khalidi (writer), Haji Mohd. Rashid b. Haji Mustafa (manager), and Haji Mohd. Yaakub b. Raja Bilah (assistant manager). The last-named was probably the Raja Yaakub thought to have been earlier associated with *Seri Perak.*]

18. AL-IMAM

Singapore; monthly; 22 July 1906–
25 December 1908
Editors: Shaykh Mohd. Tahir Jalaluddin, 1906–March 1908; Haji Abbas b. Mohd. Taha, March–December 1908

Holdings:
US°, UM+, DB°: Vol. I, Nos. 1–12
(July 1906–June 1907); II, Nos. 1–12
(July 1907–June 1908); III, Nos.
1–7 (July–Dec. 1908)
Ahmad: Vol. I, Nos. 1–12; II, Nos.
1–12; III, Nos. 1–7
DB*: Vol. I, Nos. 1, 3, 5–6, 9–11; II,
Nos. 2–4, 6, 8, 11–12; III, Nos. 1,
4, 6
Zain: Vol. I, Nos. 1, 8, 11–12; II, Nos.
2, 6–7, 9; III, Nos. 3, 5
BM*: Vol. I, No. 1

[Note: *Al-Imam* was the first of the
'religious-reform' journals in Malaysia
and Indonesia, introducing ideas which
had their origin with Shaykh Mohd.
Abduh and the *Al-Manar* circle in Cairo.
Tuan Haji Hamdan b. Shaykh Tahir has
in his possession a complete set of this
journal, which has been microfilmed by
the Dewan Bahasa dan Pustaka.]

19. UTUSAN MELAYU
Singapore; thrice-weekly until 21 Sep-
tember 1915, daily thereafter; Novem-
ber 1907–1921
Editors: Mohd. Eunos b. Abdullah, 1907–
[? 1909]; Abdul Hamid b. Miskin,
[? 1909]–[? 1914]; Mohd. Ismail b.
Abdul Kadir, [? 1914]–1918; Sayyid
Sadullah Khan, 1918–21
Holdings:
AN*, UM°, US°: Vol. [I], Nos. 5–17,
19–20, 22–3 (Nov.–Dec. 1907); [II],
Nos. 25–179 (Jan.–Dec. 1908); [III],
Nos. 181–7, 189–241, 243–7, 249–51
(Jan.–June 1909); [IV], Nos. 331–484
(Jan.–Dec. 1910); [V], Nos. 485–634
(Jan.–Dec. 1911); [VI], Nos. 635–
788 (Jan.–Dec. 1912); [VII], Nos.
789–938 (Jan.–Dec. 1913); [VIII],
Nos. 939–1092 (Jan.–Dec. 1914);
[IX], Nos. 1093–1285 (Jan.–Dec.
1915); [X], Nos. 1286–1590 (Jan.–
Dec. 1916); [XI], Nos. 1596–1614,
1616–68, 1670–1829, 1831–91 (Jan.–
Dec. 1917); [XII], Nos. 1915, 1917
(Jan. 1918); [XIV], Nos. 2536–7,
2578–90, 2596–2603, 2667–87 (Feb.,
Apr.–May, Aug. 1920)
BM*: Vol. [I], Nos. 1–23; [II], Nos.

24–62; [VI], Nos. 635–788; [VII],
Nos. 789–938; [VIII], Nos. 939–
1092; [IX], Nos. 1093–1285; [X],
Nos. 1286–1590
DB°: Vol. [IX], Nos. 1174, 1181,
1186–1208, 1213, 1216–19, 1221–2,
1233–4, 1236–8, 1240, 1245, 1247,
1250, 1252, 1258–9; [X], Nos.
1312–57, 1363–1413, 1490–1565;
[XI], Nos. 1591–1639, 1641–82,
1692–1700, 1845–64, 1866–70, 1893

[Note: From its inception until 1918,
Utasan Melayu was a Malay edition
(though much more than a translation)
of the *Singapore Free Press*. Under pres-
sure of war news, and of competition from
Lembaga Melayu (started in 1914), it
became a daily paper in September 1915.
Edited to begin with by Mohd. Eunos b.
Abdullah (who later moved to *Lembaga
Melayu*, and is often styled 'the father of
Malay journalism'), it was for many years
the principal Malay paper of substance.
It was taken over in 1918 by a group of
Indian Muslim businessmen, and its
career ended in 1921 with a sensational
libel case (Raja Shariman v. C. A.
Ribeiro & Co. Ltd., Singapore Suit No.
264 of 1921). There is some confusion
about the editorship. *TSK* (p. 132) says
that Eunos Abdullah left only in 1914 (to
go to *Lembaga Melayu*), but Nik Ahmad
('The Malay Vernacular Press', p. 16)
says that his successor, Abdul Hamid,
was editor for five or seven years, and that
the third editor, Ismail, left only in 1918.
It is worth noting that although *Utusan*
was otherwise printed entirely in Jawi,
the main news and the editorial were
reproduced on a Rumi page at the rear of
the paper. Volume numbers, as given here
for convenience, are hypothetical only.]

20. CHAHAYA MATAHARI
Singapore; weekly; October 1908–[?]
(Rumi)
Editor:
Holdings:

[Note: A Chinese revolutionary paper.
Listed under the above title in the Straits
Settlements *Blue Book* for 1908, but
referred to as *Matahari* in Chen Mong

Hock, *The Early Chinese Newspapers of Singapore, 1881–1912* (Singapore, 1967), p. 140.]

1. AL-WATAN

Singapore; fortnightly; [? month] 1909– [? 1910]

Editor:

Holdings:

[Note: The only known references to this paper occur in the Straits Settlements *Blue Books* for 1909 and 1910, where it was credited with a circulation of 1,000 copies per issue.]

2. MALAYSIA ADVOCATE

Singapore; weekly; January 1910–[?] (Rumi)

Editor: Goh Cheng Lim

Holdings:

[Note: This paper is recorded in the Straits Settlements *Blue Book* for 1910, but the only other known reference is in Song Ong Siang, *One Hundred Years' History of the Chinese in Singapore* (London, 1923), p. 348. Lim, *Newspapers Published in the Malaysian Area*, p. 175, lists a *Malayan Advocate*, of the same date, presumably in error.]

3. NERACHA

Singapore; fortnightly, then thrice-monthly, until May 1912, weekly thereafter; 15 February 1911–[? June] 1915

Editors: Haji Abbas b. Mohd. Taha; K. Anang (assistant)

Holdings:

AN*, US°, UM°: Vol. II, Nos. 28–9, 31–41, 43–7, 49–62 (Mar.–Dec. 1912); III, Nos. 63–74, 76–84, 86–100, 105–12 (Dec. 1912–Dec. 1913); IV, Nos. 113–41, 155–8 (Dec. 1913–Oct. 1914); V, Nos. 167–74, 180–7 (Jan.–May 1915)

BM*: Vol. II, Nos. 28–62; III, Nos. 63–112; IV, Nos. 113–60; V, Nos. 161–90

[Note: The editor had previously been an editor of *Al-Imam*, and the policy of *Neracha* in religious matters was similar to that of the earlier journal. In March 1913, the monthly *Tunas Melayu* was started in association with *Neracha*.]

24. TUNAS MELAYU

Singapore; monthly; March 1913–[?]

Editors: Haji Abbas b. Mohd. Taha; K. Anang (assistant)

Holdings:

[Note: Associated with the weekly *Neracha*.]

25. MAJALLAH AL-ISLAM

Singapore; monthly; [? January] 1914–[?]

Editors: K. Anang; Sayyid Mohd. al-Juneid

Holdings:

DB*: Vol. I, Nos. 5, 6, 9 (May, June, Sept. 1914); II, No. 14 (Feb. 1915)

[Note: The contents of this journal were translated from the *Islamic Review* (Woking). In 1914–15 Anang was also assistant editor of *Neracha* and *Tunas Melayu*. In 1931 he was editing an edition of the *Islamic Review* in Djakarta in Bahasa Indonesia. *TSK* (p. 140), followed by *GMP*, wrongly states that the *Majallah al-Islam* first appeared in 1918.]

26. LEMBAGA MELAYU

Singapore; daily; 1 August 1914–31 December 1931

Editor: Mohd. Eunos b. Abdullah

Holdings:

BM*: Vol. [I], Nos. 1–23, 25–111 (Aug.–Dec. 1914); [II], Nos. 112–15, 118, 121–3, 127, 130–47, 149–56, 158–417 (Jan.–Dec. 1915); [III], Nos. 418–724 (Jan.–Dec. 1916); [IV], Nos. 725–1027 (Jan.–Dec. 1917); [V], Nos. 1029–1281, 1284–1331 (Jan.–Dec. 1918); [VI], Nos. 1332–1625 (Jan.–Dec. 1919); [VII], Nos. 1626–1764, 1777–1930 (Jan.–Dec. 1920); [VIII], Nos. 1931–2081, 2083–2235 (Jan.–Dec. 1921); [IX], Nos. 2236–2537 (Jan.–Dec. 1922); [X], Nos. 2538–2840 (Jan.–Dec. 1923); [XI], Nos. 2841–2992, 2994–3146 (Jan.–Dec. 1924); [XII], Nos. 3147–3460 (Jan.–Dec. 1925); [XIII], Nos. 3461–4763 (Jan.–Dec. 1926); [XIV], Nos. 4764–5067 (Jan.–Dec.

1927); [XV], Nos. 5068–5373 (Jan.–Dec. 1928); [XVI], Nos. 5374–5677 (Jan.–Dec. 1929); [XVII], Nos. 5678–5982 (Jan.–Dec. 1930); [XVIII], Nos. 5893–6287 (Jan.–Dec. 1931)

AN*, UM+, US°: Vol. [I], Nos. 8–22, 27–9, 31, 35–7, 39–45, 54–62, 64–111; [II], Nos. 114–29, 156–88, 190–246, 249–88, 290–352; [IV], Nos. 725–89, 791–814, 816–42, 844–1028; [V], Nos. 1029–1150, 1152–1326, 1328–9; [VI], Nos. 1333, 1335–1412, 1414–20, 1422–7, 1430–58, 1460–71, 1476–1503, 1507–48, 1576–1624; [VII], Nos. 1626–1728, 1730–53, 1755–1851, 1853–1930; [VIII], Nos. 1931–2235; [IX], Nos. 2236–2537; [X], Nos. 2564–2714, 2740–2839; [XI], Nos. 2841–3146; [XII], Nos. 3147–3390, 3400–55, 3458, 3460; [XIII], Nos. 3461–4763; [XIV], Nos. 4764–5067; [XV], Nos. 5068–5373; [XVI], Nos. 5374–5677; [XVII], Nos. 5678–5892; [XVIII], Nos. 5893–6261, 6263–87

DB*: Vol. [VI], Nos. 1454–63, 1465, 1467–75, 1477–83, 1485–93, 1495, 1523, 1535–8

NL*: Vol. [XVIII], No. 6287

[Note: This was a Malay edition (though more than a translation) of the English-language *Malaya Tribune*. After the Sepoy mutiny in Singapore in 1915 it is said to have received a Government subsidy. Issue numbers are consecutive, not arranged in volumes, and the volume numbers given here are purely for convenience.]

27. WARTA PERUSAHAN TANAH

Kuala Lumpur; quarterly; [? July] 1917–[? 1941]

Editor:

Holdings:

UM*: [first series] Nos. 2, 4, 15, 16 (Nov. 1917–Apr. 1921); [second series] Vol. I, Nos. 2, 4, 5 (Mar. 1923–Jan. 1924); II, Nos. 1–4 (June 1924–Feb. 1925); III, No. 1 (May 1925); VI, Nos. 2–4 (June–Dec.

1928); VII, Nos. 1, 3 (Mar., Oct. 1929); VIII, No. 1 (Mar. 1930); XII, Nos. 1, 2 (Oct., Dec. 1934); XIV, No. 4 (Sept. 1938)

Zain: Vol. I, No. 1 (undated); IV, No. 2 (Mar. 1926); V, No. 2 (June 1927)

[Note: A journal of information produced by the F.M.S. Department of Agriculture. Although normally quarterly, it seems to have been somewhat irregular in appearance. Numbering by volumes was not started until 1923.]

28. PENGASOH

Kota Bharu (Kelantan); fortnightly until [? 1932], weekly thereafter; 11 July 1918–23 December 1937

Editors: Haji Mohd. b. Haji Mohd. Said (Dato' Bentara Jaya); Hassan b. Haji Omar; Abdul Kadir b. Ahmad (Abdul Kadir Adabi); Haji Wan Mahmud b. Haji Wan Daud; Mohd. Adnan b. Mohd Arifin

Holdings:

DB*°, UM+: Vol. II, Nos. 25–48 (June 1919–June 1920); III, Nos. 49–72 (June 1920–May 1921); IV, Nos. 73–96 (June 1921–May 1922); V, Nos. 97–120 (May 1922–Apr. 1923); VI, Nos. 121–44 (May 1923–Apr. 1924); VII, Nos. 145–68 (May 1924–Apr. 1925); VIII, Nos. 169–92 (Apr. 1925–May 1926); IX, Nos. 193–216 (Apr. 1926–Mar. 1927)

UM*: Vol. VII, Nos. 149–68; VIII, Nos. 169–92

Zain: Vol. I, Nos. 19–24 (Apr.–May 1919); II, Nos. 25–48; III, Nos. 48–72; IV, Nos. 73–96; V, Nos. 97–120; VI, Nos. 121–44; VII, Nos. 145–68; VIII, Nos. 169–72

[Note: Published by the Majlis Ugama Islam dan Isti'adat Melayu (Council of Muslim Religion and Malay Custom), Kelantan. A complete set of *Pengasoh* appears to have been lent by the Majlis Ugama in 1958 to a private individual then on the staff of the Dewan Bahasa dan Pustaka. It has not been returned or made available for microfilming. In consequence there are no copies in any public collection of the last ten pre-war years of this extremely important and influential journal.]

9. HARAPAN
Johore Bahru; irregularly; June 1919–[?]
Editor: Ariffin b. Haji Alias
Holdings:
    Zaba: Vol. I, Nos. 1–4 (June 1919, Jan., Apr., Sept. 1920)

[Note: Organ of the Persekutuan Keharapan Belia, Johore, which had been founded in 1916.]

0. SUARA PERNIAGAAN
Singapore; weekly for the first four issues, then fortnightly; 6 October 1919–[?] (Rumi and Jawi editions for first four issues, then Jawi only)
Editors: Mohd. Ismail b. Abdul Kadir; Mohd. Yusup b. Abu Bakar
Holdings:
    (Rumi edn.) BM*: Vol. I, Nos. 1–3 (Oct.–Nov. 1919)
    (Jawi edn.) BM*: Vol. I, Nos. 1–6, 8–9 (Oct. 1919–Feb. 1920)

[Note: The first three (and probably four) issues appeared in Rumi one week before their counterparts in Jawi. From No. 5, the journal appeared in Jawi only. Mohd. Ismail had edited *Utusan Melayu* for about four years, until 1918.]

1. LIDAH TERUNA
Muar; fortnightly; June 1920–[?]
Editors: Abdullah b. Mohd. Taib; Abdullah b. Abdul Wahab
Holdings:
    AN*, UM°: Vol. I, Nos. 4, 9, 18
    DB*: Vol. I, Nos. 5, 7 (Aug., Sept. 1920)
    Zaba: Vol. I, Nos. 2–18 (July 1920–Feb. 1921)
    Zain: Vol. I, Nos. 6, 9–12 (Aug., Oct.–Nov. 1920)

[Note: Organ of the Persekutuan Perbahathan Orang2 Islam (Muslim Debating Society), Muar.]

2. AL-KITAB
Kota Bharu (Kelantan); monthly; September 1920–[? December 1920]

Editors: Mohd. b. Mohd. Said (Dato' Bentara Jaya); Megat Othman b. Ali
Holdings:
    UM°: Vol. I, Nos. 1–4 (Sept.–Dec. 1920)
    DB*: Vol. I, Nos. 1–4
    Zain: Vol. I, Nos. 1–4

[Note: Although *TSK* lists this (p. 141), it was in certain respects not strictly a periodical but primarily a translation of the Kuran with commentary. A few parts only were issued.]

33. THE MUSLIM
Singapore; monthly: January 1922–[?] (English)
Editor: Kwaja Kamal-ud-Din (nominally)
Holdings:
    DB*: Vol. IV, No. 8 (Nov.–Dec. 1925)
    Zain: Vol. I, Nos. 1, 3–10 (Jan.–Dec. 1922); II, Nos. 1, 7, 9, 12 (Jan.–Dec. 1923); III, Nos. 1, 4, 7–8, 10–12 (Jan.–Dec. 1924); IV, Nos. 1–5 (Jan.–June 1925)

[Note: Organ of the Anjuman-i-Islam, Singapore, in association with the Woking (England) Muslim Mission. Kwaja Kamal-ud-Din was the founder and editor of the Woking *Islamic Review*.]

34. PANDUAN GURU
Penang; quarterly; July 1922–April 1925
Editor: Mohd. Hussein b. Abdul Rashid
Holdings:
    AN*, UM°: Vol. I, Nos. 1–4 (July 1922–Apr. 1923); II, Nos. 5–8 (July 1923–Apr. 1924); III, Nos. 9–12 (July 1924–Apr. 1925)
    Zain: Vol. I, No. 3; II, No. 8; III, Nos. 9, 11–12

[Note: Organ of the Persekutuan Guru2 Melayu, Penang, and forerunner of the *Majallah Guru* (1924).]

35. AL-HEDAYAH
Kota Bharu (Kelantan); monthly; June 1923–February 1926
Editors: Ahmad b. Ismail; Mohd. Ghazali b. Mohd. Arifin; Mohd. Adnan b. Mohd. Arifin
Holdings:

AN*: Vol. I, Nos. 1–12 (June 1923–May 1924); II, Nos. 1–12 (June 1924–May 1925)

UM°: Vol. I, Nos. 1–12; II, Nos. 1–12; III, Nos. 1–9 (June 1925–Feb. 1926)

Ahmad: Vol. I, Nos. 1–12; II, Nos. 1–12; III, Nos. 1–9

Zain: Vol. I, Nos. 1–12; II, Nos. 1–12; III, Nos. 1–9

[Note: Others concerned editorially were Abdul Rahman b. Daud, Hassan b. Haji Omar, Mohd. b. Haji Sulang, and Mahmud b. Khatib Haji Mohd. Said.]

36. SEMAIAN
Kuala Kangsar; thrice-yearly; August 1923–[?]
Editors:
Holdings:

[Note: The first journal of the Malay College, Kuala Kangsar. The only known copy of the journal, listed in *GMP*, cannot now be traced.]

37. CHENDERA MATA
Tanjong Malim; twice-yearly; 1 November 1923–[? 1941]
Editors: Various
Holdings:
AN*, UM°: Nos. 15, 19, 22, 28, 30–4 (Oct. 1930, Sept. 1932, Mar. 1934, Feb. 1937, Mar. 1938–Feb. 1940)
DB*: Nos. 5, 12, 21, 23 (Nov. 1925, Apr. 1928, Sept. 1933, Sept. 1934)
Zaba: Nos. 33–6 (1939–41)
Zain: Nos. 34–5 (Feb.–July 1940)

[Note: The journal of the Sultan Idris Training College, Tanjong Malim. A large proportion of the UM holdings of this periodical, listed in *GMP*, have since disappeared. The 'blue slip' catalogue in the Oriental Printed Books Room of the British Museum lists an unspecified holding, but this could not be traced.]

38. TETAUAN MUDA
Seremban; quarterly; December 1923–[? November 1927]
Editor: Mohd. Dom b. Hassan
Holdings:
AN*, UM°: Vol. I, No. 1 (Dec. 1923); II, Nos. 2–5 (Jan.–Oct. 1925); III,

Nos. 6–9 (Jan.–Oct. 1926); IV, Nos. 10–13 (Jan.–Nov. 1927)
DB*: Vol. II, Nos. 3–5; III, Nos. 6–9; IV, No. 11
Zain: Vol. I, No. 1; III, No. 9
Zaba: Vol. II, Nos. 4–5
BM*: Vol. I, No. 1; II, Nos. 2–5; III, Nos. 7–9; IV, Nos. 10, 12

[Note: Organ of the Persekutuan Rembau Ternakkan. As is clear from the UM holdings, there was a break in the series between December 1923 (Vol. I, No. 1) and January 1925 (Vol. II, No. 2), the issue-numbering being continuous and independent of volume.]

39. KABAR SLALU
Singapore; daily; 5 January 1924–[? 16 May 1924] (Rumi)
Editor:
Holdings:
NL*°: Vol. I, Nos. 1–109 (5 Jan.–16 May 1924)
BM*: Vol. I, Nos. 1–12, 14–21, 23–37, 39–65, 67–97, 99–105, 108–9

[Note: A Straits-born Chinese paper. Title spelt as given.]

40. MASA
Muar; monthly; January 1924–[? December 1926], June 1927–[? November 1928], April 1934–[?]
Editors: Haji Ja'afar b. Haji Mohd. Taib, Zainal Abidin b. Alias, Bahanan b. Yusop, 1924; Mohd. Noh al-Azahari, Zainal Aibidin b. Alias, 1927; Raja Mohd. Yunus b. Ahmad, 1934
Holdings:
AN*, UM°: Vol. I, Nos. 7–8, 10–12 (July–Nov. 1924); II, Nos. 13–18, 20–1, 23–4 (Dec. 1924–Nov. 1925); III, Nos. 25–36 (Dec. 1925–Oct. 1926); IV, Nos. 37–8 (Nov.–Dec. 1926); n.s. IV, Nos. 1–7, 9, 10–12 (June 1927–May 1928); V, Nos. 1–7 (June–Nov. 1928)
DB*: Vol. VI, Nos. 2, 6, 8 (May–Nov. 1934)
Zain: Vol. VI, No. 8 (Nov. 1934)

[Note: The chequered career of this journal, the organ of the Persekutuan

Suloh Pelajaran, Muar, is difficult to disentangle. It appears to have been restarted twice (in 1927, with a new Vol. IV, and in 1934), and from time to time a single monthly issue contained several issuenumbers (e.g. Vol. V, Nos. 4–7, which appeared as a single issue in November 1928).]

41. PENYULOH
Singapore; fortnightly; 30 May 1924–[? March 1925]
Editors: Mohd. Yusup b. Abu Bakar; Mohd. Hashim b. Yunus
Holdings:
AN*, UM°: Vol. I, Nos. 1–5 (May–July 1924); II, Nos. 6–19 (July 1924–Mar. 1925)
BM*: Vol. I, Nos. 1–5; II, Nos. 6–7, 9–18

[Note: Organ of the Sharikat Suloh-Menyuloh, Singapore.]

42. MAJALLAH GURU
Seremban 1924–32, Kuala Lumpur 1932–8, Penang 1939–41; monthly; 1 November 1924–December 1941
Editors: Mohd. b. Dato' Muda, 1923–32; Mohd. Yasin b. Ma'amur, 1933–8; Hassan b. Haji Abdul Manan, 1938; Zainal Abidin b. Ali, 1939–41
Holdings:
AN*, UM°: Vol. I, Nos. 1–2 (Nov.–Dec. 1924); II, Nos. 1–12 (Jan.–Dec. 1925); III, Nos. 1–12 (Jan.–Dec. 1926); IV, Nos. 1–12 (Jan.–Dec. 1927); V, Nos. 1–12 (Jan.–Dec. 1928); VI, Nos. 1–12 (Jan.–Dec. 1929); VII, Nos. 1–12 (Jan.–Dec. 1930); VIII, Nos. 1–12 (Jan.–Dec. 1931); IX, Nos. 1–12 (Jan.–Dec. 1932); X, Nos. 1–12 (Jan.–Dec. 1933); XI, Nos. 1–12 (Jan.–Dec. 1934); XII, Nos. 1–12 (Jan.–Dec. 1935); XIII, Nos. 1–12 (Jan.–Dec. 1936); XIV, Nos. 1–12 (Jan.–Dec. 1937); XV, Nos. 1–12 (Jan.–Dec. 1938); XVI, Nos. 1–12 (Jan.–Dec. 1939); XVII, Nos. 1–12 (Jan.–Dec. 1940); XVIII, Nos. 1–12 (Jan.–Dec. 1941)

DB*: Vol. I, No. 1; II, Nos. 2–12; III, Nos. 1–2, 4–10, 12; IV, Nos. 1, 3–4, 6; V, Nos. 2–3, 5–12; VII, Nos. 11–12; VIII, Nos. 1–5, 7, 9–10; IX, Nos. 6, 9–12; X, Nos. 1–8, 10–12; XI, Nos. 1–12; XII, Nos. 2–8; XIII, Nos. 10–11; XIV, Nos. 2, 9–10; XVI, Nos. 1–10, 12; XVII, Nos. 2–4, 6, 9–10; XVIII, Nos. 1, 9
Zaba: Vol. I, Nos. 1–2; II, Nos. 1–12; III, Nos. 1–12; IV, Nos. 1–12; V, Nos. 1–12; VI, Nos. 1–12; VII, Nos. 1–12; VIII, Nos. 1–12; IX, Nos. 1–12; X, Nos. 1–12; XI, Nos. 1–12; XII, Nos. 1–12; XIII, Nos. 1–12; XIV, Nos. 1–12; XV, Nos. 1–12; XVI, Nos. 1–2; XVII, Nos. 1–12
Zain: Vol. I, No. 2; III, Nos. 8–9, 12; IV, Nos. 3, 5, 6, 12; V, Nos. 8–12; X, Nos. 11–12; XI, Nos. 1, 3–11; XII, Nos. 1, 4–6, 8–11
BM*: Vol. II, Nos. 1–12; III, Nos. 1–12; IV, Nos. 1–12; V, Nos. 1–12; VI, Nos. 1–12; VII, Nos. 1–12; VIII, Nos. 1–12; IX, Nos. 1–12; X, Nos. 1–12; XI, Nos. 1–12; XII, Nos. 1–12; XIII, Nos. 1–12; XIV, Nos. 1–12

[Note: Organ of the combined Malay teachers' associations of Penang, Selangor, Negri Sembilan, and Malacca (joined later by those of Kelantan, Pahang, and Singapore), this was one of the most important intellectual monthlies circulating in the peninsula. Others on the editorial staff from time to time were Abdul Hamid b. Hassan, Mohd. Amin b. Taib (–1935), Mohd. Sharif b. Dayah (1936–), Abdul Hamid b. Haji Taha (1935–), Noordin b. Sulong, Abdullah b. Mahi (1939), and Mohd. Yusuf b. Kechil (1939–).]

43. KHABAR KAWAT MELAYU
Singapore; weekly; [? late 1924]–[? 1925] (Rumi)
Editor:
Holdings:

[Note: The Straits Settlements *Blue Books* give sales figures for 1924 as well as 1925, though possibly (as occurs in other instances) for only the last week or two of the earlier year. The 'Alphabetical

List of Oriental Periodicals' at the British Museum lists an unspecified holding for 1925, but this could not be located. *Pengasoh*, 167 (25 March 1925) reports that a Kota Bharu bookshop has sent them a 'new Singapore paper' of this name. On balance, the probability is that *Khabar Kawat Melayu* was first published at the end of 1924, perhaps in December.]

44. IDARAN ZAMAN

Penang; weekly; 15 January 1925–[? 1930]

Editors: Mohd. Yunus b. Abdul Hamid, 1925–August 1928; Othman Kalam, 1925–August 1928 (assistant)

Holdings:

AN*, UM°: Vol. I, Nos. 2–50 (Jan.–Dec. 1925); II, Nos. 1–51 (Jan.–Dec. 1926); IV, Nos. 2–5, 7–11, 16–42, 44–5, 47–50, 52 (Jan.–Dec. 1928); V, Nos. 1–2, 4–47 (Jan.–Nov. 1929); VI, No. 1 (Jan. 1930)

US°: Vol. I, Nos. 2–50; II, Nos. 1–51; V, Nos. 1–2, 4–47; VI, No. 1

NL*: Vol. III, Nos. 1–52 (Jan.–Dec. 1927); VI, No. 36 (Sept. 1930)

BM*: Preliminary issue (*bilangan permulaan*) (1 Jan. 1925); Vol. I, Nos. 1–13, 15–50

[Note: Mohd. Yunus came to Malaya from Sumatra in 1924.]

45. THE EASTERN WEEKLY REVIEW

Singapore; weekly; first series 22 January–[? 26 February] 1925, second series 13 March–[? 8 April] 1925. (First series half Rumi, half English, second series mainly English)

Editor: N. J. F. Dinger (first series only)

Holdings:

BM*: [first series] Vol. I, Nos. 1–6 (Jan.–Feb. 1925); [second series] Vol. I, Nos. 1–4 (Mar.–Apr. 1925)

[Note: Also entitled *Bintang Timor*, this largely commercial paper had two existences, as indicated, with a change of management marking the transition.]

46. AL-RAJA

Penang; monthly; 11 March 1925–[?]

Editor:

Holdings:

BM*: Vol. I, Nos. 1–11 (Mar. 1925–Mar. 1926); II, Nos. 1–3, 5 (July–Sept. 1926)

Zaba: Vol. I, No. 1; II, Nos. 1–3

Zain: Vol. IV, Nos. 3–4 (Aug.–Sept. 1928)

[Note: Organ associated with the Madrasah al-Mashhur, Penang. There appears to have been a break in publication between Volumes I and II.]

47. BINTANG SEMBILAN

Seremban; weekly; April–[? month] 1925, and January–[? month] 1926

Editor: Sayyid Ali al-Zahari

Holdings:

[Note: This journal had two brief lives, as above. The owner-manager was Abdul Hamid b. Mohd., who later edited *Chahaya Bintang* (1926).]

48. PERJUMPAAN MELAYU

Muar; fortnightly; April–[? month] 1925

Editor:

Holdings:

[Note: This journal, founded by an association called the 'Maharani Company' in April 1925, changed its name—or stopped, and began again under a new name, *Panji Melayu*—in mid year, after the Company had started a press known as the Matba'ah al-Khairiah. *TSK* (p. 153) gives the date of the first issue as 1 Shawal 1343 or 24 April 1925, but *Pengasoh*, 170 (8 May 1925), acknowledges the first three issues, which would make the starting date earlier.]

49. PANJI-PANJI MELAYU

Muar; fortnightly; [? July 1925]–[?]

Editor:

Holdings:

AN*: Vol. V, No. 94 (30 May 1929)

[Note: This was a successor to (or continuation of) the short-lived *Perjumpaan Melayu* (1925).]

50. KEMAJUAN PENGETAHUAN

Kuala Lumpur; quarterly; 22 July–
October 1925
Editor: Mohd. Isa b. Abdullah
Holdings:
   Zaba: Vol. I, Nos. 1–2 (July–Oct. 1925)
   Zain: Vol. I, No. 1

[Note: Organ of the Persekutuan Kemajuan Pengetahuan, Kuala Lumpur, this
association being the successor, under
Abdul Majid b. Zainuddin, to Zainal
Abidin b. Ahmad's Malay Literary
Society. The journal lasted for only two
issues.]

51. SUARA MALAYA

Penang; weekly; [? 19] January 1926–
[? December] 1927, 1 July 1932–[?
month] 1932
Editor: Abdul Rahman b. Jamaluddin
Holdings:
   BM*: Preliminary issue (*pendahuluan*)
   (12 Jan. 1926); Vol. I, Nos. 1–37,
   39–42, 44–50, 52 (Jan. 1926–Jan.
   1927); II, Nos. 53–71, 73–6, 78–86
   (Jan.–Sept. 1927)
   NL*: Vol. I, Nos. 1–50; II, No. 79;
   III, No. 1 (July 1932)
   AN*, US°, UM°: Vol. I, No. 52; II,
   Nos. 53–68

[Note: During its second, apparently
brief, incarnation, the paper described
itself as 'the first Malay Sunday newspaper in Malaya'. The editor died in
January 1933. Incorrectly listed in *TSK*
(p. 154) and *GMP* as *Suara Melayu*.]

52. KABAR UCHAPAN BARU

Singapore; weekly (with breaks) for most
of the first year, then fortnightly or
twice-weekly (with breaks); 4 February
1926–[?] (Rumi and English)
Editor:
Holdings:
   BM*: Vol. I, Nos. 1–14, 16, 20–35
   (Feb. 1926–Jan. 1927); II, Nos. 36–8,
   41–56 (Feb.–Dec. 1927); III, Nos.
   58–62, 65–80 (Feb. 1928–Jan. 1929);
   IV, Nos. 81–9, 91–7, 99–103, 109–17,
   120, 122, 124 (Feb. 1929–Jan. 1930)

[Note: Subtitled in English 'The Eastern
Weekly News', and described first as
'a weekly issue of the English and Romanised Malay newspaper' (*sic*) and from
No. 59 as 'The only Romanised-Malay-
newspaper of the British Malay and the
Far East', this journal appears to have
been run by and for Baba Chinese. The
'translator' was Siow Hay Yam.]

53. NUN

Yen (Kedah); fortnightly; 23 February
1926–[?], 2 September 1932–[? November 1932]
Editor: Haji Mohd. Said
Holdings:
   AN°: Vol. I, Nos. 1–9 (Feb.–June
   1926); II, Nos. 10–11 (July–Aug.
   1926)

[Note: The title is the twenty-ninth
letter of the Jawi alphabet, which prefaces
Surah LXVIII of the Kuran ('The Pen'),
and is held by some to have, in this con-
text, mystic significance. *TSK* (p. 153)
says that the first issue appeared on 1
Rejab 1344, 'or 25 December 1925'
(though 1 Rejab was in fact 15 January
1926), and there may indeed have been
a 'sample' issue (*chontoh*) around this
date, as *Pengasoh*, 8 January 1926, quoted
by *TSK*, says that 'the first number' had
just been published. *TSK* adds that after
lasting 'for only two months or so' the
journal expired, to reappear on 2 September 1932, when it published a further
two or three issues.]

54. MALAYA

Penang; monthly; May 1926–[? July
1928], and March 1931–[? May 1931]
Editor: Mohd. Yunus b. Abdul Hamid
Holdings:
   AN*, UM°: Vol. I, Nos. 1–9 (May
   1926–Jan. 1927); II, Nos. 2–9, [10],
   [11], [13] (Feb.–Sept. 1927, Oct./
   Nov., Dec. 1927, Mar./Apr./May/
   June/July 1928); III, Nos. 1–3 (Mar.–
   May 1931)
   DB*: Vol. I, Nos. 1–9; II, Nos. 2–5,
   [12]; III, No. 3
   Zain: Vol. I, No. 3; II, Nos. [10], [12]

BM*: Vol. I, Nos. 1–9; II, Nos. 2–9,
[10], [11], [12]

[Note: There was a break in publication
from July 1928 to March 1931, not two
journals of the same name as was stated
in *GMP*. Immediately prior to the break,
four unnumbered issues (here indicated
in square brackets) covered the months
October 1927 to July 1928.]

55. LEMBARAN GURU

Muar; monthly; July 1926–[?]
Editors: Yaacub b. Arshad; Haji Othman
b. Haji Mohd. Said (assistant)
Holdings:
AN*, UM°: Vol. I, Nos. 1–12 (July
1926–June 1927)
Zaba: Vol. I, Nos. 1–6

[Note: Organ of the Persekutuan Guru2
Islam, Muar. The adviser to the journal
was Haji Anda b. Haji Abdul Jama'.]

56. AL-IKHWAN

Penang; monthly; 16 September 1926–
December 1931
Editor: Sayyid Shaykh b. Ahmad al-Hadi
Holdings:
AN*, UM°: Vol. I, Nos. 1–12 (Sept.
1926–Aug. 1927); II, Nos. 1–4, 6–12
(Sept.–Dec. 1927, Feb.–Aug. 1928);
III, Nos. 1–12 (Sept. 1928–Aug.
1929); IV, Nos. 1–10, 12 (Sept.
1929–June 1930, Aug. 1930); V,
Nos. 2–12 (Oct. 1930–Aug. 1931);
VI, Nos. 1–4 (Sept.–Dec. 1931)
DB*: Vol. I, Nos. 1, 3–5, 8–9; II,
Nos. 1, 3–12; III, Nos. 1–5, 7–12;
IV, Nos. 2–12; V, Nos. 1–11; VI,
Nos. 1–2, 4
DB°: Vol. I, Nos. 1–12; II, Nos. 1–12;
III, Nos. 1–12; IV, Nos. 1–12; V,
Nos. 1–12; VI, Nos. 1–4
BM*: Vol. I, Nos. 1–10; II, Nos. 1–4,
6–7, 9–12; III, Nos. 1–12; IV, Nos.
1–12; V, Nos. 1–7, 9–12; VI, Nos.
1–4
Zaba: Vol. I, Nos. 1–10; II, Nos. 1–12;
III, Nos. 1–12; IV, Nos. 1–12; V,
Nos. 1–12; VI, Nos. 1–4
Zain: Vol. I, Nos. 1–8; II, Nos. 1–3

57. CHAHAYA BINTANG

Seremban; monthly; 1 December 1926–
[? February 1927]
Editor: Abdul Hamid b. Mohd.
Holdings:
DB*: Vol. II, No. 1 (Jan. 1927)

[Note: This journal appears to have been
devoted entirely to short stories, and
according to *TSK* (p. 157) ceased publication after three issues. The editor had
previously been owner-manager of *Bintang Sembilan*.]

58. TEROK

Pasir Puteh; monthly; 15 March 1927–[?]
Editor: Mohd. Daud b. Haji Mohd.
Salleh
Holdings:

[Note: Organ of the 'Persekutuan New
Club', Pasir Puteh, Kelantan. The
founder of the club and of the journal was
Tengku Ismail Pekerma b. Tengku
Pekerma Raja, the District Officer, and
the editor was his chief clerk. Wrongly
listed in *GMP* as *Tarok*.]

59. CHAHAYA MALAYA

Alor Star; fortnightly; 14 August 1927–[?]
Editor: Mohd. Noordin b. Haji Ali
Holdings:
BM*: Vol. I, Nos. 1–14 (Aug. 1927–
Feb. 1928)
NL*: Vol. I, No. 11

60. JASA

Johore Bahru; monthly until November
1930, then irregularly; 29 November
1927–[? September 1931]
Editor: Sayyid Zin b. Hasan al-Attas
Holdings:
AN*, UM°: Vol. I, Nos. 1–12 (Nov.
1927–Oct. 1928); II, Nos. 1–5, 7,
9–12 (Nov. 1928–Oct. 1929); III,
Nos. 1–12 (Nov. 1929–Oct. 1930);
IV, Nos. 1–6 (Nov. 1930–Sept. 1931)
DB*: Vol. I, Nos. 1–8; III, Nos. 5, 9;
IV, Nos. 2/3, 6
Zain: Vol. II, No. 1; III, No. 5
Zaba: Vol. II, No. 11

[Note: Associated with the Madrasah
al-Attas, Johore Bahru, of which Fadlullah Suhaimi was at this time Principal.
In Vol. I issues numbers 9–12 are wrongly

printed as Vol. II. Vol. IV, which appeared irregularly, is numbered 1 (Nov. 1930), 2/3 (Feb. 1931), 4/5 (June 1931), and 6 (Sept. 1931).]

61. PERDAGANGAN
Singapore; monthly; January 1928–[?] (Rumi)
Editor: Liem Khoon Liang
Holdings:
BM*: Vol. I, Nos. 1–4, 8/9, 10/11/12 (Jan.–Dec. 1928); II, Nos. 13–15, 16/17 (Jan.–May 1929)

[Note: Published (in the Indonesian spelling) by 'The Indonesia Company', run by a Singapore Chinese. Though the life of this journal is not known, there is a reference to issue No. 36 in *Al-Hikmah* (Kota Bharu), v. 217 (10 November 1938). Listed incorrectly in *TSK* (p. 159) and *GMP* as *Akhbar Perdagangan*.]

62. REAL ISLAM
Singapore; nominally monthly but very irregular; July 1928–[?] (English)
Editors: A. M. Jamaluddin, 1928–November 1929; Abdul Wahab b. Abdul Rahman, December 1929–August 1930; Sayyid M. A. Hamed b. M. A. K. Chisty, October 1930–[?]
Holdings:
BM*: Vol. I, Nos. 1–6 (July–Dec. 1928); II, Nos. 7 (Jan. 1929), 9/10/11 (Mar./Apr./May 1929), 12 (June 1929), 13 (July/Aug./Sept./Oct. 1929), 14 (Nov. 1929), 15 (Dec. 1929); III, Nos. 1/2/3 (Jan./Feb./Mar. 1930), 4/5 (Apr./May 1930), 6 (June 1930), 7 (July 1930), 8/9 (Aug./Sept. 1930), 10/11/12 (Oct./Nov./Dec. 1930); IV, Nos. 1 (Jan./Feb./Mar./ Apr./May/June 1931), 2 (July 1931), 3/4 (Aug./Sept. 1931), 5/6/7 (Oct./ Nov./Dec. 1931), 8/9/10 (Jan./Feb./ Mar. 1932), 11/12/13 (Apr./May/ June 1932), 8/9/10 [*sic*] (July/Aug./ Sept. 1932); V, Nos. 11/12/13/14/15/ 16 (Oct./Nov./Dec./1932/Jan./Feb./ Mar. 1933)

[Note: Published 'under the distinguished patronage of His Holiness Maulana Shah Muhammad Abdul Aleem Saheb Siddiqui

Al-Qadiri of Meerut City, India', this journal was markedly anti-Ahmadiyya. It is bibliographically very confused, especially in Volumes IV and V. Issue-numbers separated by diagonals (e.g. 1/2/3) indicate single issues, and the putative months of publication are indicated similarly. The holdings listed under 'Zain' in *GMP* cannot now be traced.]

63. SAUDARA
Penang; weekly until January 1932, thereafter twice-weekly; 29 September 1928– [? month] 1941
Editors: Mohd. Yunus b. Abdul Hamid, 1928–31; Sayyid Alwi b. Sayyid Shaykh al-Hadi, 1930–Feb. 1933, Mar. 1934–mid 1936; Sayyid Shaykh b. Ahmad al-Hadi, Feb. 1933–Feb. 1934 (died); Abdul Wahab b. Abdullah, Feb. 1933–Mar. 1934; Shaykh Mohd. Tahir Jalaluddin, Mar.–Sept. 1934; Abdul Majid b. Sabil, mid 1936–June 1939; Mohd. Amin b. Nayan, late 1939– 1941
Holdings:
AN*, US°, UM°: Vol. I, Nos. 2–24, 26–34, 36–51 (Oct. 1928–Sept. 1929); II, Nos. 52–73, 75–103 (Sept. 1929– Sept. 1930); III, Nos. 104–17, 119– 52 (Oct. 1930–Sept. 1931); IV, Nos. 153–7, 160, 180–206, 208–43 (Sept.– Nov. 1931, Feb.–Sept. 1932); V, Nos. 244–69, 277–331, 333–44 (Oct. 1932–Sept. 1933); VI, Nos. 346–79, 381–432, 434–6, 439–45, 447 (Oct. 1933–Sept. 1934); VII, Nos. 448–62, 464–503, 505–6, 508–21, 523–31, 533–48 (Oct. 1934–Sept. 1935); VIII, Nos. 549–612, 614–51 (Oct. 1935–Sept. 1936); IX, Nos. 652–68, 670–736 (Oct. 1936–Sept. 1937); X, Nos. 737–61, 771–8, 839–40 (Oct.–Dec. 1937, Feb., Oct. 1938); XI, Nos. 841–7, 906 (Oct. 1938, May 1939); XII, Nos. 964–71, 974–80 (Jan.–Feb. 1940); XIII, Nos. 1041–2, 1045, 1047–52 (Oct. 1940)
BM*: Vol. IV, Nos. 168–243 (Jan.– Sept. 1932); V, Nos. 244–344 (Sept. 1932–Sept. 1933); VI, Nos. 345– 447 (Sept. 1933–Sept. 1934); VII, Nos. 448–548 (Sept. 1934–Sept.

1935); VIII, Nos. 549–651 (Oct. 1935–Sept. 1936); IX, Nos. 652–736 (Oct. 1936–Sept. 1937); X, Nos. 737–840 (Oct. 1937–Oct. 1938); XI, Nos. 841–938 (Oct. 1938–Sept. 1939); XII, Nos. 939–63 (Oct.–Dec. 1939), 1007–15 (June 1940); XIII, Nos. 1041–55, 1057–64, 1066–77 (Oct. 1940–Jan. 1941); XIV, Nos. 1078–92 (Jan.–Feb. 1941)

[Note: *Saudara* was founded by Sayyid Shaykh b. Ahmad al-Hadi, who exercised considerable editorial influence over it until his death in 1934. Printed at the Jelutong Press until (? August) 1939, the paper changed hands managerially when the press was sold at that time. Publishers (*penerbit*) for the remaining two years were listed, successively, as Raja Othman b. Mohd. Noor, S. A. O. Alsagoff, Shaykh Abdul Rahman b. Abu Bakar, and Mohd. b. Che' Ambi. The small collection of editorial pages (extracts ranging in length from two to six pages) in the National Library of Singapore is without issue-numbers. In so far as these issues (listed fully in *GMP*) supplement those in the Arkib Negara Malaysia, they are as follows: Vol. I, No. 25; Vol. IV, 19 July 1932; Vol. V, 10 January, 20 and 24 May, and 14 June 1933; and Vol. XIII, 17 December 1940.]

64. DUNIA MELAYU
Penang; monthly; 20 December 1928–[? July 1930]
Editor: Dibab b. Haji Mohd. Salleh
Holdings:
   AN*, UM°: Vol. I, Nos. 1–12 (Dec. 1928–Nov. 1929); II, Nos. 1–8 (Dec. 1929–July 1930)
   DB*: Vol. I, No. 10
   Zaba: Vol. I, Nos. 1–4, 6
   BM*: Vol. I, Nos. 1–12; II, Nos. 1–8

[Note: Others involved were Jusoh Abdullah (manager), Mohd. Ali Ahmad al-Johari and Mohd. Nur b. Abdul Rahman (*pengurus*), and Hasan b. Abdullah (special assistant). Listed incorrectly in *GMP* as *Majallah Dunia Melayu*.]

65. THE TORCH
Kota Bharu (Kelantan); monthly; [? 1928] (? English)
Editor:
Holdings:

[Note: Published by Old Boys of the Majlis Ugama Islam English School. Cf. *Al-Hikmah*, VII, 299 (6 July 1940).]

66. WARTA NEGERI
Kuala Lumpur; weekly until 17 May 1931, twice-weekly thereafter; 27 May 1929–[?] (Rumi)
Editor: Mu'id (later entitled Dato' Raja di-Raja Rembau)
Holdings:
   BM*: [Vol. I], Nos. 1–53 (May 1929–May 1930); [II], Nos. 54–106 (June 1930–May 1931); [III], Nos. 107–16 (May–June 1931)
   AN*: [Vol. I], Nos. 33–53; [II], Nos. 54–84
   NL*: [Vol. I], No. 1; [III], No. 127 (Oct. 1931)

[Note: Described itself as 'the only romanised Malay weekly paper in the Federated Malay States'.]

67. WARTA PINANG
Penang; fortnightly; 1 September 1929–[?]
Editor: Haji Abdul Aziz
Holdings:
   AN*, UM°: Vol. I, Nos. 1–3 (Sept.–Oct. 1929)
   BM*: Vol. I, Nos. 1–3

[Note: Others concerned were Harun Shah (manager) and Tengku Sayyid Nasir (secretary).]

68. LIDAH BENAR
Klang; weekly; 3 September 1929–[?]
Editors: Mohd. Ali Ahmad al-Johari; Mohd. Damih b. Ibrahim
Holdings:
   AN*: Vol. I, Nos. 27–43 (Mar.–July 1930); II, Nos. 1–50 (Sept. 1930–Sept. 1931); III, Nos. 1–49 (Sept. 1931–Sept. 1932); IV, Nos. 1–15 (Sept.–Dec. 1932)
   NL*: Vol. I, Nos. 1–2; II, No. 30

BM*: Vol. I, Nos. 27–43; II, Nos. 1–50; III, Nos. 1–49; IV, Nos. 1–31 (Sept. 1932–Apr. 1933)

[Note: Mohd. Said b. Ali al-Malakawi was manager.]

69. PETRA
Kota Bharu (Kelantan); fortnightly; 1 October 1929–[? December 1929]
Editor: Abdul Kadir b. Ahmad (Abdul Kadir Adabi)
Holdings:
NL*: Vol. I, No. 1 (Oct. 1929)

[Note: Believed to have run for six issues only, or possibly—if irregular in appearance—for six months.]

70. SEMANGAT ISLAM
Penang; monthly; 1 November 1929–[? January 1931]
Editor: Abdul Latif Hamidi
Holdings:
AN*, UM°: Vol. I, Nos. 1–12 (Nov. 1929–Oct. 1930); II, Nos. 13–15 (Nov. 1930–Jan. 1931)
DB*: Vol. I, Nos. 2–12; II, Nos. 13–15
Zaba: Vol. I, Nos. 1–12; II, Nos. 13–15
BM*: Vol. I, Nos. 1–12; II, Nos. 13–15

71. PUNCHA PERTIKAIAN ULAMA ISLAM
Penang; monthly; November 1929–[? November 1930]
Editor:
Holdings:
UM*: Vol. I, Nos. 1–5, 8–12 (Nov. 1929–Oct. 1930); II, No. 13 (Nov. 1930)
Zaba: Vol. I, Nos. 1–12; II, No. 13
BM*: Vol. I, Nos. 1–3, 8–12; II, No. 13

[Note: Though this appeared serially, it was in fact a publication in parts of a translation into Malay of the *Bidayatu'l-Mujtahid Wa Nihayatu'l-Muktsaid*, a jurisprudential work by the philosopher Ibn Rushd (Averroes).]

72. MAJALLAH AL-KAMALIAH
Kota Bharu (Kelantan); fortnightly; 1 January 1930–[?]

Editors: Haji Noh b. Ali; Shaykh Ali b. Kassim (assistant)
Holdings:
AN*, UM°: Vol. I, Nos. 2–8 (Jan.–Apr. 1930)

[Note: Haji Noh was a lawyer (*peguam*) and a teacher in the Madrasah Muhammadi, Kota Bharu. The journal was managed by Umar b. Haji Taib, owner of Al-Kamaliah Press.]

73. WARTA MALAYA
Singapore; daily; 1 January 1930–December 1941
Editors: Onn b. Ja'afar, 1930–December 1933; Sayyid Alwi b. Sayyid Shaykh al-Hadi, 1933–February 1934; Sayyid Hussein b. Ali Alsagoff, February 1934–August 1941; Ibrahim b. Haji Ya'akub, August–December 1941
Holdings:
AN*°, UM+, US°: Vol. I, Nos. 2–36, 38–150, 168–266, 268–307 (Jan.–Dec. 1930); II, Nos. 1–98, 100–202, 203–305 (Jan.–Dec. 1931); V, Nos. 1–288, 290–300, 304–6 (Jan.–Dec. 1934); VI, Nos. 1–74, 76–227, 229–31, 233, 235–52, 254–74, 276–7, 279–304 (Jan.–Dec. 1935); VII, Nos. 151–305 (July–Dec. 1936); IX, Nos. 51–74, 152–77, 205–28, 256–80 (Mar., July, Sept., Nov. 1938); X, Nos. 100–25, 235, 237–44, 246–54, 276–84, 287 (May, Oct.–Dec. 1939); XI, Nos. 76–152, 232–5, 237, 239, 243–5, 249, 254, 256, 271–82, 309 (Apr.–Dec. 1940); XII, Nos. 76–100, 129–53 (Apr., June 1941)
BM*: Vol. I, Nos. 1–307; II, Nos. 1–305; V, Nos. 1–306; VI, Nos. 1–303; VII, Nos. 1–305; VIII, Nos. 1–306; IX, Nos. 1–307; X, Nos. 1–307; XI, Nos. 1–309; XII, Nos. 1–180
NL*: Vol. III, Apr. 9, 20; May 5, 6, 13, 19, 20, 21, 26, 28, 30; June 1, 4, 6, 10, 11, 13, 15, 16, 17, 28, 30; July 6, 8; Aug. 2, 3, 5, 6; Sept. 7 (1932); IV, Feb. 6, 28; Mar. 2, 8, 13, 16, 18, 22, 23, 27, 30; Apr. 21, 22, 25, 26, 27, 28, 29; May 2, 3, 4, 5, 8, 10, 18, 22, 24; June 1, 2, 10, 13, 15, 16, 20, 24, 26, 27, 28, 29, 30; July 1, 3, 4, 5, 6,

7, 8, 10, 11, 12, 13, 14, 15, 17, 18, 19,
20, 21, 22, 24, 25, 26, 27, 29, 31;
Aug. 1, 2, 3, 4, 12, 19, 23, 24, 25, 26,
27, 29, 31; Sept. 11, 12, 13, 14, 16,
18, 19; Oct. 9, 12, 17, 18, 19, 20, 21,
24, 26, 29, 30, 31; Nov. 1, 8, 16, 22,
30; Dec. 6, 7, 8, 9, 11, 12, 22, 23
(1933)

[Note: The office of *Utusan Melayu*,
Kuala Lumpur, has Vol. IV, Nos. 229–
304 (Oct.–Dec. 1933). The collection of
editorial pages (extracts ranging from two
to six pages in length) in the National
Library of Singapore is without issue-
numbers. Details of the complete National
Library holding in this form were given,
by date order, in *GMP*, but it has now
been thought sufficient to provide details
of only those two volumes which are
missing from the other two main holdings
of this paper. It is to be hoped that the
very complete British Museum holdings
of this important metropolitan daily can
before long be microfilmed.]

74. CHAHAYA TIMOR
Penang; weekly; 4 January 1930–[?]
Editors: Othman Kalam; Haji Abdul
Aziz (assistant)
Holdings:
BM*: Vol. I, No. 1 (Jan. 1930)

[Note: The holding listed under UM in
GMP cannot now be traced. A Haji
Abdul Aziz had been editor of the fort-
nightly *Warta Pinang* in 1929.]

75. FAJAR SARAWAK
Kuching; fortnightly; 1 February 1930–
[?]
Editor: Mohd. Rakawi b. Yusop
Holdings:
NL*: Vol. I, No. 1 (Feb. 1930)

[Note: Published by the Sharikat Putera
Sarawak. Others involved were Haji
Mohd. Daud b. Abdul Ghani, Mohd.
Johari b. Anang, Haji Abdul Rahman b.
Haji Kassim, and Mohd. Awi b. Anang.
This is the only Malay-language paper
known to have been published in 'British
Borneo' before 1941.]

76. PANDUAN TERUNA
Ipoh; weekly; 21 February 1930–[?]
Editors: Sayyid Othman b. Shaykh;
Ahmad Nawawi b. Mohd. Ali (assistant)
Holdings:
NL*: Vol. I, Nos. 3, 19 (Mar., July
1930)

77. TEMASEK
Singapore; monthly; 1 March 1930–
[? September 1930]
Editor: Haji Mohd. Kassim Bakry
Holdings:
AN*, UM°: Vol. I, Nos. 1–7 (Mar.–
Sept. 1930)
Zaba: Vol. I, Nos. 1–7
BM*: Vol. I, Nos. 1–7

[Note: Organ associated with the Madrasah al-Juneid, Singapore, founded in
1927 by Sayyid Abdullah b. Omar al-
Juneid and run by Fadlullah Suhaimi.
The editor was an Indonesian who had
been active in the nationalist movement
in the Netherlands East Indies.]

78. CHAHAYA
Muar; ? monthly; 2 March 1930–[?]
Editor:
Holdings:
Zaba: Vol. I, No. 1 (Mar. 1930)

79. KENCHANA
Kota Bharu (Kelantan); monthly for first
year, fortnightly thereafter; April 1930–
[? month] 1931
Editor: Mohd. Sa'ad b. Haji Muda
(Sa'ad Shukri)
Holdings:
AN*, UM°: Vol. I, Nos. 1, 3, 5, 7–10
(Apr. 1930–Jan. 1931)

[Note: The Malay Studies Department
of the University of Malaya had, in 1961,
a microfilm of a manuscript fifteen-part
history of Kelantan, being a copy of a
series of articles in this journal, written
by the editor, and later (1962) published
in book form. According to *TSK* (p. 168)
Kenchana ceased publication shortly
after becoming a fortnightly.]

80. BULAN MELAYU
    Johore Bahru; monthly June 1930 to
    May 1932, and from May 1934 to
    [? February] 1938, then quarterly from
    [? January] 1938, and two-monthly
    from January 1941; June 1930–[? month]
    1941
    Editor: Hajah Zin bte Sulaiman
    Holdings:
       AN*, UM°: Vol. I, Nos. 1–12 (June
       1930–Apr. 1931); II, Nos. 1–12 (May
       1931–Apr. 1932); III, Nos. 1 (May
       1932), 3 (June 1935), 33 [9] (Nov.
       1935); [IV], Nos. 43–4 (Oct.–Nov.
       1936); [V], No. 53 (Aug. 1937);
       [VI], No. 62 (Aug. 1938)
       DB*: Vol. I, Nos. 1–5, 8–12; II, Nos.
       1–5, 7–9, 11; III, Nos. 2–3 (May–
       June 1935), 28–33 [4–9] (July–Nov.
       1935), [34 (10)] (Nov. 1935); [IV],
       Nos. 45–6 (Dec. 1936–Jan. 1937)
       Zaba: Vol. I, Nos. 1–12; II, Nos. 1–12;
       III, Nos. 1 (May 1932), 2–11 (May
       1935–Jan. 1936); [Vol. ?], Unnum-
       bered three issues bound in with the
       quarterly *Idaman*, Vol. I, Nos. 1–3
       (Jan.–July 1940)

    [Note: Journal of the Persekutuan Guru2
    Perempuan Melayu, Johore. Its biblio-
    graphical history is very confused. There
    was a break in publication between Vol.
    III, No. 1 (May 1932) and Vol. III, No. 2
    (May 1935), and shortly after this
    enumeration by volume was abandoned
    for cumulative numbering by issue,
    apparently reckoning from Vol. I, No. 1,
    but further confused by discrepancies
    between Muslim and Christian months.
    From January 1940 it ceased to appear
    independently, but was issued together
    with the journal of the Persekutuan
    Guru2 Melayu Johor, *Idaman*.]

81. KATOK-KATOK
    Muar; monthly; August 1930–[?]
    Editors: Mohd. Alias; Hashim al-Ruji
       (assistant)
    Holdings:

    [Note: Others concerned were Ismail
    Ja'afar (publisher) and Kassim Salleh
    (manager).]

82. BINTANG PRANAKAN
    Singapore; weekly; 11 October 1930–
    [? June 1931] (Rumi)
    Editor:
    Holdings:
       BM*: Vol. I, Nos. 1–34 (Oct. 1930
       June 1931)

    [Note: Published by Wan Boon Seng,
    this described itself as 'the only Straits-
    born Chinese romanized-Malay weekly
    journal in British Malaya'. The title, like
    the content, represents Baba Chinese
    spelling.]

83. SUARA
    Kota Bharu (Kelantan); weekly; 12
       March 1931–[?]
    Editor: Noh b. Ali Bafdzal
    Holdings:
       NL*: Vol. I, Nos. 1–3 (Mar. 1931)

    [Note: Organ of the Sharikat al-Ittihad
    al-Islamiah, a trading company or educa-
    tional establishment in Kota Bharu. The
    manager of *Suara* was Ahmad b. Isa
    Banjari.]

84. IDARAN MASA
    Kuala Trengganu; fortnightly; May–
       [? month] 1931
    Editor: Mohd. Hassan Riau
    Holdings:
       NL*: Vol. I, No. 3 (July 1931)

    [Note: This journal is thought to have
    appeared only briefly, and was probably
    succeeded by *Lidah Watan*, under the
    same editorship. It was the first periodical
    to be published in Trengganu.]

85. SINAR MALAYA
    Ipoh; monthly; July 1931–[?] (Rumi)
    Editor: Ahmad Noor b. Abdul Shukor
    Holdings:
       AN*, UM°: Vol. I, Nos. 1–3 (July–
       Sept. 1931)

86. LIDAH WATAN
    Kuala Trengganu; fortnightly; 13 August
       1931–[?]
    Editor: Mohd. Hassan Riau
    Holdings:

87. DEWASA
    Penang; twice-weekly; 19 October 1931–
    [?]
    Editors: Mohd. Yunus b. Abdul Hamid;
    Haji Abdul Ghani b. Haji Hassan
    (assistant)
    Holdings:
    BM*: Vol. I, Nos. 1–7, 9–12, 14–20
    (Oct.–Dec. 1931)
    AN*°, UM+, US°: Vol. II, Nos. 11–13,
    15–23, 25–30, 32–3 (Feb.–May 1932)
    NL*: Vol. I, Nos. 1, 4

    [Note: The manager was Haji Mohd.
    Araf b. Haji Ali.]

88. KABAR BINTANG TIMOR NEWS
    Singapore; ? thrice-weekly; 20 October
    1931–[?] (Rumi)
    Editor:
    Holdings:
    NL*: Vol. I, No. 1 (Oct. 1931)

    [Note: A Straits-born Chinese journal,
    owned by Siow Hay Yam (earlier
    associated with *Kabar Uchapan Baru*)
    and O. S. Key.]

89. KANAK-KANAK
    Singapore; weekly; 13 November 1931–
    [?]
    Editor: Abdul Karim b. Ismail
    Holdings:
    AN*, US°, UM°: Vol. I, Nos. 2–13
    (Nov. 1931–Feb. 1932)
    NL*: Vol. I, No. 4
    BM*: Vol. I, Nos. 1–13

    [Note: A children's paper, managed by
    Ahmad b. Haji Abdul Rahman.]

90. MAJLIS
    Kuala Lumpur; twice-weekly until Janu-
    ary 1935, thrice-weekly until 1939,
    thereafter daily; 17 December 1931–
    December 1941
    Editors: Abdul Rahim Kajai, 1931–Jan.
    1935; Othman Kalam, Jan. 1935–1939;
    Ibrahim b. Haji Yaacob, 1939–41;
    Salehuddin, 1941
    Holdings:
    AN*: Vol. I, Nos. 1, 6–38 (Jan.–May
    1932); II, Nos. 39–138 (May 1932–
    Apr. 1933); III, Nos. 139–238 (Apr.

1933–Apr. 1934); IV, Nos. 239–339
(Apr. 1934–Apr. 1935); V, Nos. 340–
439 (Apr. 1935–Mar. 1936); VI, Nos.
440–539 (Mar. 1936–Mar. 1937);
VII, Nos. 540–688 (Mar. 1937–Feb.
1938); VIII, Nos. 689–838 (Mar.
1938–Feb. 1939); IX, Nos. 839–978
(Feb.–Dec. 1939); X, Nos. 979–1298
(Dec. 1939–Dec. 1940)
DB°: Vol. IV, Nos. 314–39; V, Nos.
340–439; VI, Nos. 440–539; VII,
Nos. 540–688; VIII, Nos. 689–818
BM*: Vol. I, Nos. 1–38; II, Nos. 39–
138; III, Nos. 139–238; IV, Nos.
239–339; V, Nos. 340–439; VI, Nos.
440–539; VII, Nos. 540–688; VIII,
Nos. 689–838; IX, Nos. 839–978;
XI, Nos. 1301–1445, 1448–1523,
1531–84 (Jan.–Dec. 1941)

[Note: The Singapore National Library
holdings of editorial cuttings listed in
GMP do not supplement the holdings in
Kuala Lumpur, and accordingly have not
been reproduced here.]

91. BAHTERA
    Penang; twice-weekly; 1 January 1931–
    [? August 1932]
    Editor: Othman Kalam
    Holdings:
    AN*, US°, UM°: Vol. I, Nos. 2–12,
    14–16, 18–22, 24–56 (Jan.–Aug.
    1932)
    BM*: Vol. I, Nos. 1–12, 14–16, 18–22,
    24–56

    [Note: The manager was Mohd. Idrus b.
    Haji Suleiman.]

92. PERKHABARAN DUNIA
    Singapore; daily; 9 February–March
    1932
    Editors: Mohd. Eunos b. Abdullah;
    N. M. Ali Munshi (assistant)
    Holdings:
    AN*, US°, UM°: Vol. I, Nos. 2–45
    (Feb.–Mar. 1932)
    BM.: Vol. I, Nos. 1–45

    [Note: Mohd. Eunos b. Abdullah had been
    editor for seventeen years of the daily
    Lembaga Melayu, which ceased publica-
    tion in December 1931. This attempt to

found a replacement on his own account failed after six weeks.]

93. KEMAJUAN MELAYU

Singapore; monthly; April 1932–[?]
Editor: Suleiman b. Ahmad
Holdings:
> BM*: Vol. I, Nos. 1–4 (Apr.–July 1932)
> DB*: Vol. I, No. 5 (? Aug. 1932)

[Note: This was the first of perhaps seven, usually ephemeral, light magazines produced and edited by Suleiman b. Ahmad in the mid 1930s, the others being *Tanah Melayu, Dunia Sekarang,* (? *Melayu Muda,* 1935), *Shorga Dunia, Melayu Muda,* 1936, and (? *Penggeli Hati*). Several were disapproved of and banned by state religious officials, as allegedly salacious. The holdings of *Kemajuan Melayu* listed under UM in *GMP* cannot now be traced.]

94. SUARA BENAR

Malacca; twice-weekly; 2 September 1932–[? February 1933]
Editor: Haji Mohd. Taib b. Haji Mohd. Hashim
Holdings:
> AN*, US°, UM°: Vol. I, Nos. 2–51 (Sept. 1932–Feb. 1933)
> NL*: Vol. I, Nos. 1–2, 4, 8, 11, 14–15, 17, 20–8, 31–2, 34–51
> BM*: Vol. I, Nos. 1–51

[Note: The only Malay newspaper to be published in Malacca during the period covered by this bibliography.]

95. AL-JOHORIAH

Johore Bharu; monthly; October 1932–[?]
Editor: Mohd. Salleh b. Alwi
Holdings:
> Zaba: Vol. I, No. 1 (Oct. 1932)

[Note: Published by Al-Jama'ah al-Islamiah al-Johoriah for the Pakatan Islam Johor.]

96. BUMIPUTERA

Penang; daily; 5 January 1933–[? 1936]
Editors: Othman Kalam and Abdul Wahab b. Abdullah (for Vol. I only); Mohd. Amin (subsequently)
Holdings:
> AN*, US°, UM°: Vol. I, Nos. 22–95, 130–1, 135–200, 203–22, 224–36, 238–71, 273–90, 292–9, 301–4 (Feb. 1933–Jan. 1934); II, Nos. 2–297 (Jan.–Dec. 1934)
> NL*: Vol. I, No. 6
> BM*: Vol. I, Nos. 1–3, 5–117, 119–23, 125, 127–236, 238–304; II, Nos. 1–254, 256–97, 299; III, Nos. 2–9 (Jan. 1935)

[Note: Abdul Wahab Abdullah, named as publisher as well as editor for Volume I, had previously been on the editorial board of the Indonesian/Malay monthly *Seruan Azhar* in Cairo in the 1920s, and an editor of *Saudara*. The British Museum holding includes an additional special issue, unnumbered, for Hari Raya, 5 January 1935.]

97. PEMIMPIN MELAYU

Penang; weekly; 11 July 1933–[?]
Editor:
Holdings:
> AN*, US°, UM°: Vol. I, Nos. 2–11, 18–20, 22–5 (July–Dec. 1933); II, Nos. 26–50 (Jan.–July 1934)
> BM*: Vol. II, Nos. 26–7, 29–53

[Note: The publisher was Omar Khan.]

98. TANAH MELAYU

Singapore; irregularly to mid 1933, monthly from March 1934 to October 1936, and again from January 1937; March 1933–[?]
Editor: Suleiman b. Ahmad
Holdings:
> BM*: Vol. I, Nos. 1–4 (Mar., Apr., June, Dec. 1933); [II], Nos. 5–16 (Mar. 1934–Feb. 1935); [III], Nos. 17–28 (Mar. 1935–Feb. 1936); [IV], Nos. 29–36, 37–8 (Mar.–Oct. 1936, Jan.–Feb. 1937); [V], Nos. 39, 41, 43–4 (Mar.–Aug. 1937); [Vol. ?], No. 1 (Jan. 1940)
> AN*, UM°: Vol. I, Nos. 1–3; [II], Nos. 5–8, 10–11, 13; [III], Nos. 21–7; [IV], Nos. 31, 33, 36; [V], No. 39
> Zaba: Vol. [II], Nos. 8–10

[Note: According to *TSK* (p. 180), this

journal was prohibited from entry into Johore and Trengganu. Volume numbers were not assigned after the first four issues, and have been added here for convenience only. The 1940 issue in the British Museum is of the same format, and under the same editorship, as the original journal, but is numbered 1.]

99. BERITA SEKOLAH

Penang; nominally quarterly; March 1934–[?]

Editors: Ashaari b. Mohd. Isa; Mohd. Shahid b. Haji Abdullah; Othman b. Mohd. Ali

Holdings:
> DB*: Vol. II, Nos. 4–5 (July–Sept. 1935); V, No. 12 (Jan. 1938)
> BM*: Vol. II, No. 4; III, No. 7 (July 1936)
> Zaba: Vol. I, Nos. 1–2 (Mar.–July 1934); II, No. 4

[Note: Associated at first with the Chowrasta Malay School, Penang, this journal was by 1936 appearing under the auspices of 'the Malay schools of Penang and Seberang Prai'. In 1936 the manager was Raja Mohd. Nurdin b. Raja Deli (then Assistant Inspector of Malay Schools for the area), and in 1938 Mohd. Yusup b. Kechik, followed by Mohd. Nur b. Ibrahim, both of the Education Office, Penang.]

100. AL-HIKMAH

Kota Bharu (Kelantan); thrice-monthly until 1936, weekly until 1941, then fortnightly; 1 April 1934–December 1941

Editor: Ahmad b. Ismail

Holdings:
> Ahmad: Vol. I, Nos. 1–36 (Apr. 1934–Mar. 1935); II, Nos. 37–80 (Apr. 1935–Mar. 1936); III, Nos. 81–132 (Apr. 1936–Mar. 1937); IV, Nos. 133–85 (Apr. 1937–Mar. 1938); V, Nos. 186–237 (Apr. 1938–Mar. 1939); VI, Nos. 238–89 (Apr. 1939–Mar. 1940); VII, Nos. 290–341 (Mar. 1940–Mar. 1941); VIII, Nos. 342–58 (Apr.–Dec. 1941)

> AN*, UM°: Vol. I, Nos. 1–14, 16–18, 20–1, 23, 28; II, Nos. 49–55, 57–74, 76, 78, 80; III, Nos. 81, 83–4, 86–8, 92–3, 109, 119–20, 131–2; IV, Nos. 139, 161; V, Nos. 187, 192, 205, 212–13, 217–37; VI, Nos. 238–89; VII, Nos. 290–300, 302–37; VIII, Nos. 343–4
> DB*: Vol. IV, Nos. 152–85; V, Nos. 190–209, 211–37; VI, Nos. 238–89; VII, Nos. 290–341
> Zain: Vol. I, Nos. 18, 24, 27, 30, 32–4; II, No. 40; VIII, No. 353

[Note: A lively and imaginative news magazine, dealing with Kelantan, peninsular, and general affairs. The owner and editor, a writer and translator of some note, had previously been responsible for *Al-Hedayah* (1923–6).]

101. THE STORY TELLER

Singapore; fortnightly; [? June] 1934–[?] (Rumi)

Editor:

Holdings:
> BM*: Vol. I, Nos. 8–13, 15 (Oct. 1934–Jan. 1935); II, Nos. 1–18 (Jan.–Oct. 1935)

[Note: Not strictly a periodical, this appears to have consisted solely of the publication in serial parts of the Baba Chinese 'Cherita Dahulu-Kala bernama Beng Leh Koon atau Cha Boh Chai Sang di Zaman Guan Teow'.]

102. DUNIA SEKARANG

Singapore; fortnightly; 14 July 1934–[?]

Editor: Suleiman b. Ahmad

Holdings:
> AN*°, UM+, US°: Vol. I, Nos. 2–13, 16–27 (Sept. 1934–Oct. 1935)
> BM*: Vol. I, Nos. 1–9

[Note: According to *TSK* (pp. 181–2), this journal was prohibited from entry into Johore and Trengganu. There was a break in publication between the first issue (July 1934) and the second (September 1934).]

103. TAJA PENGHIBORAN
Muar; quarterly; [? September] 1934–[?]
Editor: Sayyid Abdul Kadir b. Mohd.
b. Yahya
Holdings:
DB*: Vol. I, No. 4 (June 1935)

[Note: Journal of the 'pehak ahli2 persuratan, Muar Club, Bandar Maharani'.]

104. PANDUAN
Kuala Kangsar; monthly; November 1934–[?]
Editor: Haji Mohd. Noor Fa'iz
Holdings:
DB*: Vol. I, Nos. 1–6 (Nov. 1934–Apr. 1935)
UM*: Vol. I, Nos. 1–2
Zain: Vol. I, No. 5

[Note: Associated with the Madrasah al-Idrisiah, Kuala Kangsar.]

105. CHAHAYA SINGAPURA
Singapore; monthly; 1 December 1934–[?]
Editor: A. K. Daharoz
Holdings:
BM*: Vol. I, Nos. 1–7 (Dec. 1934–June 1935)
DB*: Vol. I, Nos. 2–6

[Note: The holding listed under 'Hamdan' in *GMP* (Vol. I, Nos. 5, 6, 11), was given to UM, but together with UM's own then holding (Vol. II, No. 13) cannot now be traced.]

106. NERACHA
Muar; fortnightly; 1 December 1934–[?]
Editor: Abdul Ghani b. Abdullah
Holdings:
DB*: Vol. I, Nos. 1–8 (Dec. 1934–Mar. 1935)

[Note: The manager was Hassan b. Mohd.]

107. LEMBAGA MALAYA
Singapore 1934–7, Johore Bahru 1938–41; weekly; 10 December 1934–1941
Editors: Onn b. Ja'afar, 1934–mid 1936; Sayyid Alwi b. Sayyid Shaykh al-Hadi, mid 1936–1941

Holdings:
AN*°, UM+: [Vol. I], Nos. 2, 4, 5, 17–18, 22, 27–9, 31–44, 46–52 (Dec. 1934–Dec. 1935); [II], Nos. 54–69, 71–82, 84–7, 89–90, 92–4, 96–7, 99–103 (Dec. 1935–Nov. 1936); III, No. 2 (Dec. 1936); IV, Nos. 5–45 (Jan.–Oct. 1938); V, Nos. 39, 42, 46, 52 (Sept., Oct., Dec. 1939); VI, Nos. 10, 14–16, 21, 24–5, 28, 30, 34, 37–53 (Feb.–Dec. 1940); VII, Nos. 3, 6, 11–14, 16, 19–25, 34–6, 40–1, 43–4, 50–1 (Jan.–Dec. 1941)
DB*: [Vol. I], Nos. 3–5, 8–34; [II], Nos. 76, 104; III, Nos. 1, 10, 22, 27, 30, 36 (Dec. 1936, Feb., May, June, Aug. 1937); IV, Nos. 28, 32; V, Nos. 8, 15, 25, 32; VII, Nos. 4–5, 12, 15–16, 19–21, 29, 36, 41, 43, 45–7, 49, 50
BM*: [Vol. I], Nos. 1–52; [II], Nos. 53–104; III, Nos. 5–16

[Note: The first two volumes were numbered consecutively, by issue, without volume numbers.]

108. KESAH MALIK SAIF BIN ZI YAZIN
Alor Star; fortnightly; [? 1934]
Editor: Ismail H. M. Said
Holdings:
BM*: Nos. 1, 3 (no date)

[Note: Not strictly a periodical, this was a publication in fortnightly parts of a well-known traditional story from the Persian. The British Museum catalogue hypothesizes the date of publication as 1934, on what evidence is not clear.]

109. MELAYU MUDA
Singapore; fortnightly; 1 January 1935–[?]
Editor: [? Suleiman b. Ahmad]
Holdings:
BM*: Vol. I, No. 1 (Jan. 1935)

[Note: *TSK* (p. 183), referring to *Majallah Guru* of February 1935, lists a *Pemuda Melayu* of approximately this date, and was followed by *GMP*. The author of *TSK* had not himself seen a journal of this name, and it now seems

likely, from the British Museum holding, that either he or *Majallah Guru*
mistook the title for *Melayu Muda*. Cf.
also the second incarnation of *Melayu
Muda*, published weekly in July 1936.]

110. PEDOMAN ISLAM
    Seberang Prai; fortnightly; 19 April
    1935–[?]
    Editor: Haji Abdul Aziz
    Holdings:
        DB*: Vol. I, Nos. 1–3, 5 (Apr.–June
        1935)
        Zain: Vol. I, Nos. 1, 3–4
        BM*: Vol. I, Nos. 4–5

[Note: *TSK* (p. 183) gives the place as
Bagan Tua Kechil, Seberang Prai. It
was wrongly stated as Penang in *GMP*.
A Haji Abdul Aziz had earlier been
editor of *Warta Pinang* (1929) and
assistant editor of *Chahaya Timor*
(1930).]

111. DEWAN PEREMPUAN
    Singapore; fortnightly; 1 May 1935–[?]
    Editor: Raja Mohd. Eunos b. Raja Haji
    Ahmad
    Holdings:
        DB*: Vol. I, Nos. 1–5 (May–July
        1935)
        BM*: Vol. I, Nos. 1–3
        Zain: Vol. I, No. 1

[Note: This journal was wrongly listed
as *Dewan Wanita* in *GMP*.]

112. WARTA AHAD
    Singapore; weekly; 5 May 1935–
    December 1941
    Editors: Sayyid Hussein b. Ali Alsagoff,
    1936–August 1941; Ibrahim b. Haji
    Yaacob, August–December 1941
    Holdings:
        AN*, US°, UM°: Vol. [I], Nos. 1,
        6–7, 11, 13–14, 16–22, 25–35 (May–
        Dec. 1935); [II], Nos. 36–9, 41–84,
        86–7 (Jan.–Dec. 1936); [III], Nos.
        88–135, 137–9 (Jan.–Dec. 1937);
        [IV], Nos. 140–62, 164–91 (Jan.–
        Dec. 1938); [V], Nos. 192–203,
        209–15, 217, 219–22, 224–5, 230,
        232, 234–6, 238, 240–4 (Jan.–Dec.
        1939); [VI], Nos. 247–55, 259,

261–2, 264–6, 268–72, 273–7, 279–
84, 286–92, 295–6 (Jan.–Dec.
1940); [VII], Nos. 298–308, 311–
17, 325–7, 330–8, 341–6 (Jan.–May,
July–Dec. 1941)
        DB*: [Vol. II], Nos. 55, 67–80, 84–5
        (May, Aug.–Dec. 1936); [III],
        Nos. 91–2, 109, 113, 118 (Jan., May,
        June, July 1937); [IV], Nos. 140–2,
        144–6, 148–56, 158–78, 184–5,
        190–1 (Jan.–Dec. 1938); [V], Nos.
        193, 195–8, 218, 221–3, 225, 234
        (Jan.–Feb., July–Aug., Oct. 1939);
        [VI], Nos. 246, 248, 253, 255–9,
        261, 263–4, 266–8, 271 (Jan., Mar.–
        July 1940); [VII], Nos. 297, 299–
        300, 302, 304–20, 322–3 (Jan.–
        July 1941)
        BM*: [Vol. I], Nos. 1–35 (Jan.–Dec.
        1935); [II], Nos. 36–87; [III], Nos.
        88–139; [IV], Nos. 140–91; [V],
        Nos. 192–244; [VI], Nos. 245–96;
        [VII], Nos. 297–326 (Jan.–Aug.
        1941)

[Note: This was the Sunday edition of
Warta Malaya. The Arkib Negera has
recently acquired a confused, incomplete, and partly damaged holding cover-
ing the period May 1937 to April 1941,
which it has not been possible to list.]

113. NEGRI
    Seremban; monthly; June 1935–[?]
    Editor: Abdul Hamid b. Mohd.
    Holdings:
        BM*: Vol. I, Nos. 1–2 (June–July
        1935)

114. AL-HIKMAH
    Kepala Batas; ? frequency; July 1935–[?]
    Editor:
    Holdings:

[Note: Associated with the former pupils
of the Madrasah al-Ma'arif al-Wataniah,
Kepala Batas, Provinces Wellesley. May,
like *Al-Kitab* (1920) and *Puncha Pertikaian Ulama Islam* (1929), have been
not a journal proper but wholly or
primarily the publication in parts of
a religious text or texts.]

115. LIDAH IBU
Singapore; ? weekly; 1 September
1935–[?]
Editor: Sayyid Mohd. b. Zain Alsagoff
Holdings:
[Note: The holding listed under UM
in *GMP* cannot now be traced.]

116. USAHA MELAYU
Seremban; fortnightly; 1 September
1935–[?]
Editor: Abdul Ghani b. Tahir
Holdings:
BM*: Vol. I, Nos. 1–5 (Sept.–Nov.
1935)
AN*, UM°: Vol. I, Nos. 1–2

117. MEDAN LAKI2
Singapore; weekly; 27 September 1935–
[?]
Editor: Sayyid Ahmad Hussain Dahlan
Holdings:
BM*: Vol. I, Nos. 1–14 (Sept. 1935–
Jan. 1936)
AN*, UM°: Vol. I, Nos. 1–3, 5, 9
DB*: Vol. I, Nos. 13–14
[Note: Describes itself as the first Islamic
illustrated weekly in Malaya.]

118. KAHIDUPAN DUNIA AKHIRAT
Singapore; fortnightly until August
1936, monthly from November 1936;
1 October 1935–[? December 1936]
Editor: Mohd. Ali Abduh
Holdings:
BM*: Vol. I, Nos. 2–22 (Oct. 1935–
Aug. 1936); II, Nos. 23–4 (Nov.–
Dec. 1936)
AN*: Vol. I, Nos. 6–11, 9, 20–1
UM°: Vol. I, Nos. 6–11
[Note: Succeeded in August 1937 by
Seruan Kebajikan, under the same
editorship. Not to be confused with the
later *Dunia Akhirat* (1936).]

119. LEMBAGA
Singapore 1935–8, Johore Bahru 1938–
41; daily; 8 October 1935–1941
Editors: Onn b. Ja'afar, 1935–6; Sayyid
Alwi b. Omar Albar, late 1936–mid
1939; Sayyid Alwi b. Sayyid Shaykh
al-Hadi, mid 1939–1941

Holdings:
BM*: [Vol. I], Nos. 1–303 (Oct.
1935–Oct. 1936); II, Nos. 1–132
(Oct. 1936–Mar. 1937)
AN*: Vol. III, Nos. 71–294 (Jan.–
Sept. 1938), No. ? (Dec. 1938)
NL*: Vol. V, No. 1
[Note: The holdings for this important
metropolitan daily are more deficient
than for any other newspaper of similar
stature.]

120. MAJALLAH PEMUDA
Batu Pahat; monthly; November 1935–
[?]
Editor: Daud b. Suleiman
Holdings:
BM*: Vol. I, Nos. 1–2 (Nov.–Dec.
1935)
Zaba: Vol. I, Nos. 1–2

121. WIHDATU'L-MADARIS
Penang; quarterly; November 1935–[?]
Editor: Shaykh Mohd. Husain Rafi'e
Holdings:
[Note: Published from the Madrasah
al-Mashhur, Penang, for the Jama'ah
Guru2 Ugama Semenanjong Melayu,
and described (on the cover) as 'the first
magazine of its kind, published quarterly
by the teachers of the Arabic schools'.]

122. GENUINE ISLAM
Singapore; monthly; January 1936–[?]
(English)
Editor: Hafiz Mohd. Rahman Ansari
Holdings:
Zain: Vol. I, Nos. 9–12 (Sept.–Dec.
1936); II, Nos. 2–5 (Aug.–Nov.
1937); III, Nos. 1–6, 8 (Jan.–June,
Aug. 1938); IV, Nos. 6–7 (June–
July 1939); VI, No. 1 (Jan. 1941)
[Note: Journal of the All-Malaya Mus-
lim Missionary Society, Singapore.]

123. SAUJANA
Singapore; annually; January 1936–[?]
Editors: Othman b. Hassan; Mahmud
b. Ahmad
Holdings:
Zaba: Nos. 3 (Dec. 1937), 4 (Oct.
1938), 6 (Nov. 1940)

[Note: The annual of the Persekutuan Guru2 Melayu Singapura. The holding listed under UM in *GMP* cannot now be traced.]

124. THE MUSLIM MESSENGER
Singapore; monthly; April 1936–[?] (English)
Editor: [? Ismail b. Haji Ali]
Holdings:
BM*: Vol. I, Nos. 1–5 (Apr.–Aug. 1936)

[Note: Ismail b. Haji Ali may have been publisher as well as (or rather than) editor.]

125. SHORGA DUNIA
Singapore; monthly; 1 March–[? September] 1936
Editor: Suleiman b. Ahmad
Holdings:
BM*: Vol. I, Nos. 1–5 (Mar.–Sept. 1936)
AN*, US°, UM°: Vol. I, Nos. 4–5

[Note: There was a break in publication between No. 4 (June) and No. 5 (September).]

126. PENGHIBORAN
Ipoh; fortnightly; 1 April 1936–[?]
Editor: Ahmad Nawawi b. Mohd. Ali
Holdings:
BM*: Vol. I, Nos. 1–10 (Apr.–Aug. 1936)

[Note: Appears to have been primarily devoted to short stories of a homiletic kind. The editor, well known in religious reform circles, had previously been assistant editor of *Panduan Teruna* (1930). The holding listed under UM in *GMP* cannot now be traced.]

127. MELAYU MUDA
Singapore; weekly; 13 July 1936–[?]
Editor: Suleiman b. Ahmad
Holdings:
BM*: Vol. I, Nos. 1–3 (July 1936)
AN*, US°, UM°: Vol. I, Nos. 2–3

[Note: See also the fortnightly of the same name published in January 1935, of which this appears to be a later incarnation. Each is described (in English) as 'A Malay [fortnightly/ weekly] newspaper devoted to reformation and progress of the Malays'.]

128. AL-ISLAM
Penang; monthly; July 1936–[?]
Editors: Yusof Ahmad Lubis; Ibni Hassan (assistant)
Holdings:
Zaba: Vol. I, No. 1 (July 1936)

[Note: Published by the Pejabat al-Islam, Penang, and managed by Haji Ibrahim Akibi.]

129. DUNIA AKHIRAT
Singapore; fortnightly; July 1936–[?]
Editor:
Holdings:
AN*, UM°: Vol. I, Nos. 2–3, 6, 8, 19, 23 (Aug.–Nov. 1936, Feb., June 1937)

[Note: Publication appears to have become irregular towards the end of the extant series. Not to be confused with *Kahidupan Dunia Akhirat* (1935).]

130. PERSAHABATAN
Penang; thrice-monthly until October 1936, weekly thereafter; 21 July 1936–[?]
Editors: Mohd. Yunus b. Abdul Hamid; Mohd. Zain b. Haji Ibrahim (assistant)
Holdings:
AN*, UM°: Sample issue (*perchontohan*) (30 June 1936); Vol. I, Nos. 1–21 (Aug. 1936–Jan. 1937)
DB*: Sample issue; Vol. I, Nos. 2–3, 7–9, 11–16, 18, 20–3
BM*: Sample issue; Vol. I, Nos. 1–19

[Note: Others concerned were Haji Mohd. Taib b. Mohd. Saman (publisher) and Mohd. Ali b. Mohd. al-Rawi (manager).]

131. MEDAN AL-ISLAM
Singapore; weekly; 14 August 1936–[?]
Editor: Sayyid Ahmad Hussain Dahlan
Holdings:
BM*: Vol. I, No. 1 (Aug. 1936)

[Note: The publisher was M. Mohd. Kassim. Sayyid Ahmad had earlier edited the weekly *Medan Laki2*.]

132. DUNIA PEREMPUAN
Singapore; monthly; July 1936–[?]
Editor: Mohd. Ali Abduh
Holdings:
BM*: Vol. I, Nos. 1–3 (July, Sept., Oct. 1936)

[Note: There was a break in publication between the first and second issues, as indicated.]

133. WARTA JENAKA
Singapore; weekly; 7 September 1936–[? December] 1941
Editors: Sayyid Hussein b. Ali Alsagoff, 1936–August 1941; [? Ibrahim b. Haji Yaacob, August–December 1941]
Holdings:
AN*, US°, UM°: Vol. I, Nos. 1–17 (Sept.–Dec. 1936); II, Nos. 18–34, 38, 41–53, 55–8, 60–9 (Jan.–Dec. 1937); III, Nos. 70–101, 103–21 (Jan.–Dec. 1938); IV, Nos. 122–32, 138–9, 141–5, 147–50, 152–5, 158, 161, 170 (Jan.–Dec. 1939); V, Nos. 174–5, 178, 180, 183–217 (Mar.–Oct. 1940); VI, Nos. 230–2, 236, 238, 259–61 (Mar., Aug.–Oct. 1941)
DB*: Vol. I, Nos. 1, 3–17; II, Nos. 18–24, 26–32, 34–7, 39–54, 56, 59–69; IV, Nos. 126–7, 145, 150, 152–3, 158–9, 170; V, Nos. 174–6, 180, 196, 218; VI, Nos. 252–5
BM*: Vol. I, Nos. 1–2, 4–17; II, Nos. 18–69; III, Nos. 70–121; IV, Nos. 122–73; V, Nos. 174–225; VI, Nos. 226–52

[Note: Weekly magazine associated with *Warta Malaya*.]

134. PENGGELI HATI
Singapore; monthly; [? September] 1936–[?]
Editor: [? Suleiman b. Ahmad]
Holdings:

135. SUARA KALAM
Penang; monthly; 15 or 25 October 1936–[?]
Editor: Abdul Wahab Zain
Holdings:

[Note: There is a discrepancy between the dates given on and inside the cover of the first and only known issue. The holdings listed for both UM and Zain (from which this information was obtained) in *GMP* cannot now be traced.]

136. CHAHAYA ISLAM
Singapore; fortnightly; February 1937–[?]
Editor: Haji Ahmad Dahlan Langkat
Holdings:

137. WARTA PERAK
Ipoh; weekly; 13 March 1937–[?]
Editors: Ahmad Noor b. Abdul Shukor; Abdul Rahman al-Yobi
Holdings:
NL*: Sample issue (6 Feb. 1937); Vol. I, Nos. 1, 8–9 (Mar., May 1937)

[Note: Ahmad Noor had previously been editor of *Sinar Malaya* (1931).]

138. LIDAH PERSAUDARAAN
Penang; fortnightly; 16 March 1937–[?]
Editor: Mohd. Zain b. Haji Ibrahim
Holdings:

[Note: Founders and publishers were Abdul Hamid Haji Mohd. and Haji ·Ibrahim b. Aman. Mohd. Zain had previously been assistant editor of *Persahabatan*.]

139. SERUAN KEBAJIKAN
Singapore; monthly; August 1937–[?]
Editor: Mohd. Ali Abduh
Holdings:

[Note: According to *TSK* (p. 194) this was the successor to *Kahidupan Dunia Akhirat* (1935), which had ceased publication some six months earlier. Mohd. Ali had previously been editor of that and of *Dunia Perempuan* (1936).]

140. VOICE OF ISLAM
Singapore; monthly; October 1937–[?]
Editor:
Holdings:
BM*: Vol. I, Nos. 1, 3–4 (Oct., Dec. 1937/Jan. 1938, Feb./Mar. 1938); II, No. 1 (Jan./Feb. 1939)
Zain: Vol. I, Nos. 2, 4

[Note: Dedicated to Siddiqi al-Qadiri, and under the patronage of Tengku Temenggong Ahmad of Johore. Though describing itself as a monthly, the existing issues are clearly irregular.]

141. WARTA KINTA
Ipoh; weekly until May 1938, daily from September 1939 onwards; 24 December 1937–10 May 1938, and 25 September 1939–[? 1941]
Editors: Raja Mansor b. Raja Abdul Kadir; Haji Yang Hamzah (assistant)
Holdings:
AN*, UM°: Vol. I, Nos. 1–12, 14–17 (Dec. 1937–May 1938); II, Nos. 3, 10, 17 (Sept., Oct. 1939, Jan. 1940); III, Nos. 71–291 (Jan.–Sept. 1940); IV, Nos. 1–78 (Sept.–Dec. 1940)

[Note: For the first seventeen issues (with a break between No. 9, 18 February 1938, and No. 10, 22 March 1938) the paper was a weekly. It ceased publication in May 1938, and resumed as a daily in September 1939. The paper, at least in its later incarnation, had some association with the daily *Times of Malaya*, also published in Ipoh. The editor, Raja Mansor, a Sumatran Malay, had previously edited *Pewarta Deli* and the *Deli Courant* in Medan, and was well known as author of numerous rather erotic novels.]

142. TEMASHA
Kuala Lumpur; fortnightly; 19 February 1938–[?]
Editor: Abdul Aziz Hassani
Holdings:
DB*: Vol. I, No. 1 (Feb. 1938).

143. SEMANGAT GURU
Ipoh; thrice-yearly; 20 March 1938–[?]
Editor: Othman b. Mohd. Akib
Holdings:
Zain: Vol. I, No. 3

[Note: Journal of the Persekutuan Guru2 Melayu Perak.]

144. SINARAN KELANTAN
Kota Bharu (Kelantan); ? quarterly; March 1938–[? June 1938]
Editor: Mohd. Yusop b. Salleh
Holdings:
AN*, UM°: Nos. 1–2 (Mar.–June 1938)

[Note: Whether or not this was intended to be a periodical, it seems likely that only two issues were published.]

145. PASPAM
Penang; monthly; 15 June 1938–[? month] 1941
Editor: Mohd. Arifin b. Ishak
Holdings:
UM*: Vol. II, No. 6 (Sept. 1939); III, Nos. 1–12 (May 1940–Apr. 1941); IV, Nos. 1–7 (May–Nov. 1941)
Zaba: Vol. II, Nos. 1–12 (May 1939–Apr. 1940); III, Nos. 1–10; IV, Nos. 2–4, 6

[Note: This was also known as *Pemberita Pejabat Paspam*, and was the journal of the Persaudaraan Sahabat Pena Malaya. In Vol. II there appear to be two distinct issues numbered 11. See also *Taman Paspam*, the annual.]

146. SUARA PENA
Singapore; monthly; 1 September 1938–[? month] 1939
Editor: Mohd. Yaacob Baginda
Holdings:
AN*, UM°: Vol. I, Nos. 1–3, 5 (Sept. 1938–Jan. 1939)

[Note: This journal was associated with the Singapore branch of the Persaudaraan Sahabat Pena Malaya. It was succeeded in May 1939 by *Pancharan Pena*.]

147. MAJALLAH AL-RIWAYAT
Kota Bharu (Kelantan); fortnightly until May 1939, thereafter monthly; 1 November 1938–[? month] 1939
Editor: Haji Ishak b. Lutfi Omar
Holdings:
DB*: Vol. I, No. 4 (Dec. 1938)

[Note: Devoted initially to short stories, but from No. 14 onwards included general articles as well.]

148. MAJALLAH CHERITA
Penang; monthly; 1 November 1938–[?]
Editors: Mohd. Arifin b. Ishak; Aminah bte Abdul Jalil (assistant)
Holdings:
   AN*, UM°: Nos. 1–3 (Nov. 1938–Feb. 1939)
   Zaba: Nos. 3–8 (Feb.–Aug. 1939)

[Note: As the name implies, a short-story magazine.]

149. PEMANDANGAN
Singapore; monthly; 1 February 1939–[?]
Editor: Shaykh Hassan Hajab
Holdings:

150. SAHABAT
Penang; thrice-weekly; 15 February 1939–[? 1941]
Editors: Sayyid Ahmad b. Shaykh; Ahmad Boestamam; Mohd. Samin b. Taib; Ahmad Nur b. Abdul Shukur; Husin Baba; Mohd. Zain b. Haji Ibrahim
Holdings:
   AN*, UM°: Vol. I, Nos. 80, 115, 135–6, 138–51 (Aug., Nov. 1939, Feb. 1940); II, Nos. 1–15, 17, 20 (Feb.–Mar. 1940)
   NL*: Vol. I, No. 1 (Feb. 1939)
   DB*: Vol. II, No. 110/111 (Nov. 1940)

[Note: A major change seems to have taken place in the management of this paper in mid 1940. At the outset the publisher was Haji Abdul Aziz b. Shaykh Rahmat (who from October 1939 also published *Siasat*), but by late 1940 the paper was being published by Mohd. Tamim b. Sutan Deman. Similarly, not all the editors listed above served at the same time, and it seems probable that the four last-named were associated with the paper after mid 1940. The Singapore National Library holdings listed in *GMP* cannot now be traced.]

151. CHAHAYA NEGERI
Kuala Pilah; fortnightly; 1 April–June 1939
Editor: Ismaon b. Mohd. Yunus
Holdings:
   US°: Vol. I, No. 4 (May 1939)
   Zain: Vol. I, Nos. 1, 5 (Apr., June 1939)

[Note: This was the journal of the Persatuan Perniagaan, Kuala Pilah. Printed at Ipoh, it stopped publication in June 1939 to transfer to Kuala Pilah, but was never resumed. The holding listed under UM in *GMP* cannot now be traced.]

152. PANCHARAN PENA
Singapore; fortnighly; 1 May–[? July] 1939
Editor: Ja'afar b. Abdul Rahman
Holdings:
   DB*: Vol. I, No. 2 (May 1939)
   Zain: Vol. I, No. 6 (July 1939)

[Note: Journal associated with the young members of the Singapore branch of the Persaudaraan Sahabat Pena Malaya, and supported, according to *TSK* (p. 200), by Malay students overseas. It succeeded the journal *Suara Pena*.]

153. SUARA MALAYSIA
Penang; weekly; 8 May 1939–[?] (Rumi)
Editor: Shamsuddin Yahya
Holdings:
   DB*: Vol. I, Nos. 1–10, 13–14 (May–Aug. 1939)

[Note: Journal of the Lembaga Pustaka Melayu, Penang. Others concerned were Mohd. Samin b. Taib (managing director), Mohd. Amin (manager), and Rentah b. Siarap (publisher).]

154. UTUSAN MELAYU
Singapore; daily; 29 May 1939–[? January 1942]
Editor: Abdul Rahim Kajai
Holdings:
   BM*: Vol. I, Nos. 2–39, 41–51, 53–86, 88–91, 93–170, 172–85 (May–Dec. 1939); II, Nos. 2–260, 262–311 (Jan.–Dec. 1940); III, Nos. 312–541 (Jan.–Sept. 1941)

AN*, UM°, US°: Vol. I, Nos. 112, 118 (Oct. 1939); II, Nos. 8, 30 (Jan., Feb. 1940)

Utusan Melayu Office, Kuala Lumpur: Vol. I, Nos. 1–29 (May–June 1939)

[Note: Because it is hoped that the nearly complete British Museum holdings of this important paper will shortly be filmed and become available for use in Malaysia and Singapore as well as elsewhere, details of the cuttings of editorial pages held by the National Library, Singapore, and detailed in full in *GMP*, are not given here.]

155. BINTANG MALAYA

Singapore 1939, Muar 1940–1; monthly; 1 June 1939–[? December 1941]

Editor: Haji Abdul Hamid Fadzil al-Muari

Holdings:

Zain: Vol. I, Nos. 2, 4–5 (July–Oct. 1939); II, Nos. 11–12 (May, June 1941)

Zaba: Vol. I, Nos. 2, 4, 6 (July–Nov. 1939); II, No. 18 (Dec. 1941)

DB*: Vol. II, Nos. 10, 12 (Sept. 1940, June 1941)

[Note: Stopped publication after the November 1939 issue (Vol. I, No. 6) and started again, in Muar, in June 1940 (Vol. I, No. 7). Stopped publication a second time after the September 1940 issue (Vol. I, No. 10) and restarted in May 1941 (Vol. I, No. 11). The journal appears to have had some connection with the Kuliah al-Firdaus school in Singapore.]

156. AL-IHSAN

Kuala Pilah; fortnightly; 15 July 1939– [?]

Editor: Shamsuddin Yahya

Holdings:

[Note: Journal of the Lembaga al-Ihsan, Kuala Pilah. The editor and the publisher (Rentah b. Siarap) had previously been associated in these capacities with the Penang *Suara Malaysia*.]

157. THE MALAY COLLEGE MAGAZINE

Kuala Kangsar; annually; September 1939–1940 (English)

Editor:

Holdings:

[Note: The second Malay College magazine (the first was *Semaian*, 1923). Two issues only before the war.]

158. SIASAT

Penang; monthly; 15 October 1939–[?]

Editor: Haji Abdul Aziz b. Shaykh Rahmat

Holdings:

[Note: Published in association with *Sahabat* (1939).]

159. UTUSAN ZAMAN

Singapore; weekly; 5 November 1939– January 1942

Editor:

Holdings:

AN*, UM°: Vol. I, Nos. 1–61 (Nov. 1939–Dec. 1940); II, Nos. 1–3, 5–18, 20–2, 25–53 (Jan. 1941–Jan. 1942)

[Note: The Sunday edition of *Utusan Melayu*.]

160. IDAMAN

Batu Pahat; quarterly until January 1941, then irregularly; 1 January 1940– [? September] 1941

Editor: Abdul Hamid b. Markam

Holdings:

DB*: Vol. I, Nos. 1–14 (Jan.–Oct. 1940); II, Nos. 5–9 (Jan., Apr., May, June, Sept. 1941)

[Note: Journal of the Persekutuan Guru2 Melayu Johor, Batu Pahat. The woman's magazine *Bulan Melayu*, organ of the Persekutuan Guru2 Perempuan Melayu, Johore, was issued with it.]

161. SEMANGAT MELAYU

Batu Pahat; monthly; 8 February 1940–[?]

Editor: Ahmad b. Haji Taib

Holdings:

[Note: The editor was a frequent contributor to the Malay press under the pseudonym 'Ahab'.]

162. TAMAN PASPAM
Batu Pahat; annually; February 1940–[?]
Editor: Mohd. Arifin b. Ishak
Holdings:
    UM*: No. 1 (Feb. 1940)
    Zaba: No. 1

[Note: The annual of the Persaudaraan Sahabat Pena Malaya.]

163. DEWAN PERGAULAN
Penang; monthly; [? March] 1940–[?]
Editor:
Holdings:

164. THE MODERN LIGHT
Johore Bahru; monthly; May 1940–[? September] 1941 (English)
Editor: Haji Abdul Latiph b. Haji Abdul Majid
Holdings:
    UM°: Vol. I, Nos. 1–5, 7–12 (May 1940–Apr. 1941)
    Zain: Vol. I, Nos. 1–5, 7–12

[Note: Described itself as 'the first and only Malay national organ in English'. Although Haji Abdul Latiph was effective editor, his father, Haji Abdul Majid, took a large part in running the journal.]

165. SERUAN IHYA
Taiping; ? monthly; [? April] 1941–[?]
Editor:
Holdings:
    Zain: Sample issue (Mar. 1941)

[Note: Organ associated with the Madrasah al-Ihya Abu Sharif, near Taiping.]

166. FILM MELAYU
Singapore; monthly; [? May] 1941–[?]
Editor:
Holdings:

[Note: Published by H. Abdullah Ja'afar, according to *Al-Hikmah*, VIII, 344 (15 May 1941).]

167. SUARA ISLAM SA-MALAYA
Ipoh; bi-monthly; [? May] 1941–[?] (Rumi, also English and Tamil)
Editor: Ahmad Noor b. Abdul Shukor
Holdings:

[Note: Published by K. Sultan Marican, according to *Al-Hikmah*, VIII, 344 (15 May 1941).]

168. MASTIKA
Singapore; monthly; 1 June–December 1941
Editor: Abdul Rahim Kajai
Holdings:
    AN*, UM°: Vol. I, Nos. 1–7 (June–Dec. 1941)
    Zain: Vol. I, No. 3

[Note: A literary periodical associated with *Utusan Melayu*.]

169. MAJALLAH ROMANS
Singapore; monthly; [? June] 1941–[?]
Editor:
Holdings:

[Note: Second issue referred to in *Al-Hikmah*, VIII, 349 (1 Aug. 1941).]

170. WARTA PERANG
Singapore; weekly; 2 October 1941–[?]
Editor:
Holdings:
    NL*: Vol. I, No. 6 (Nov. 1941)

[Note: An official journal of propaganda.]

171. SURAT PERKHABARAN MELAYU
Singapore; daily; [? November] 1941–[?]
Editor:
Holdings:
    DB*: Unnumbered (17–22, 24–6 Nov., 1–6, 8, 10 Dec. 1941)

[Note: This was a news sheet published by the Department of Information, Government of the Straits Settlements.]

172. BELENGGU PERKASEHAN
Ipoh; monthly; [? 1941]
Editor:
Holdings:

[Note: Romantic short stories. The holding listed under UM in *GMP* cannot now be traced.]

173. CHAHAYA TIMOR
Kuala Trengganu; weekly; [? 1941]
Editors: Haji Mohd. Saleh b. Haji Awang; Abdul Kadir Adabi (Abdul Kadir b. Ahmad); Ibrahim Fikri b. Mohd.
Holdings:
[Note: This is said to have been an official, or semi-official, organ of information.]

SECTION TWO: ARABIC

174. AL-HUDA

Singapore; weekly; 25 May 1931–
[? June 1934]
Editor: Sayyid A. W. Jilani
Holdings:
   BM*: Vol. I, Nos. 1–51 (May 1931–
   May 1932); II, Nos. 52–102 (May
   1932–May 1933); III, Nos. 103–38
   (May 1933–June 1934)
   UM*: Vol. I, Nos. 2–18, 20, 33–51;
   II, Nos. 52–102; III, Nos. 103–38

[Note: This paper stopped publication
between issues No. 127 (25 December
1933) and No. 128 (20 April 1934).]

175. AL-'ARAB

Singapore; weekly until April 1934,
twice-monthly from August 1934;
20 October 1931–April 1934, 1 August
1934–[? month] 1935
Editor: Sayyid Ahmad b. Omar Ba Faqih
Holdings:
   BM*: Vol. I, Nos. 1–53 (Oct. 1931–
   Oct. 1932); II, Nos. 54–68, 90–7
   (Oct. 1932–Jan. 1933, Aug.–Oct.
   1933); III, Nos. 98–102, 107–9,
   114–21 (Nov. 1933–Oct. 1934); IV,
   Nos. 122–5, 127 (Nov. 1934–Jan.
   1935)
   UM°: Vol. I, Nos. 1–53; II, Nos.
   54–97; III, Nos. 98–121
   UM*: Vol. I, Nos. 15–29, 31–8, 40–
   53; II, Nos. 54–68, 90–7; III, Nos.
   98–102, 107–9, 114–21; IV, Nos.
   122–3, 125–6

[Note: This paper was owned by Sayyid
Hussein b. Ali Alsagoff. Numbering by
volume was discontinued after issue
No. 65, but has been entered here for
convenience.]

176. AL-GISAS

Singapore; fortnightly; 11 February
1932–[?]
Editor: Sayyid Faraz b. Talib (until

June 1932); Sayyid A. W. Jilani (from
June 1932)
Holdings:
   BM*: Vol. I, Nos. 1–12, 14–20, 22–33
   (Feb. 1932–July 1933)
   UM*: Vol. I, Nos. 2–12, 14–27,
   29–33

177. AL-NAHDAH AL-HADRAMIYAH

Singapore; monthly; January 1933–[?]
Editor: Sayyid Taha b. Abu Bakar
Alsagoff
Holdings:
   BM*: Vol. I, Nos. 1–8 (Jan.–Dec.
   1933)
   UM°: Vol. I, No. 4

[Note: The eight known issues appeared
as follows: Jan., Mar./Apr., May, June/
July, Aug., Sept., Oct., Nov./Dec. 1933.]

178. AL-SHA'B AL-HADRAMI

Singapore; fortnightly for first four
issues, thereafter monthly; 17 March
1933–[? February 1934]
Editor: Sayyid Faraz b. Talib
Holdings:
   BM*: Vol. I, Nos. 1–16 (Mar. 1933–
   Feb. 1934)
   UM*: Vol. I, Nos. 2–9, 11–16

179. AL-JAZA'

Singapore; fortnightly; April 1934–[?]
Editor: Sayyid Faraz b. Talib
Holdings:
   UM*: Vol. I, Nos. 2–3 (Apr.–May
   1934)

180. AL-HISAB

Singapore; fortnightly; January 1935–[?]
Editor: Sayyid Faraz b. Talib
Holdings:
   BM*: Vol. I, No. 1 (Jan. 1935);
   II, No. [? 2] (Apr. 1936)
   UM*: Vol. II, No. [? 2]

181. AL-MAJD AL-'ARABI
Singapore; fortnightly; 20 March 1935–
[? September 1935]
Editor: Sayyid Faraz b. Talib
Holdings:
BM*: Vol. I, Nos. 1–13 (Mar.–Sept. 1935)
UM*: Vol. I, Nos. 2–13

182. SAWT HADRAMAWT
Singapore; thrice-monthly in 1935, twice-monthly in 1940 and 1941; April 1935–[? month 1935], [? June 1940]–[? month] 1941
Editor: Sayyid Taha b. Abu Bakar Alsagoff
Holdings:
BM*: Vol. I, Nos. 1–5, [? 7–9, 11/12] (Apr.–July 1935); II, Nos. 4–6, 8, 10–11, 21–3 (Aug.–Nov. 1940, June–Aug. 1941); III, No. 25 (Sept. 1941)
UM*: Vol. I, Nos. 1–5

[Note: Somewhat erratic numbering of volumes and issues makes it difficult to disentangle the history of this publication, but there appears to have been a break in continuity between, probably, 1935 and 1940.]

183. AL-SALAM
Singapore; monthly until October 1937, thereafter thrice-monthly; [? February] 1937–[?]
Editor: Sayyid Ahmad b. Omar Ba Faqih
Holdings:
BM*: Vol. I, Nos. 5–24 (June 1937–July 1938); II, Nos. 25–42, 45, 47–53, 55–64 (July 1938–Dec. 1939)
UM*: Vol. I, Nos. 5–12; Unnumbered issue (Feb. 1940)

[Note: Volume and issue numbering are as given.]

184. AL-MASHHUR
Singapore; ? frequency; [? December 1938]
Editor: Sayyid Mohd. b. Zain Alsagoff
Holdings:
[Note: The only known reference to this paper, in *Al-Hikmah* (Kota Bharu), v, 221 (8 December 1938), records the appearance of what seems to be the first issue. *Al-Hikmah*, III, 81 (2 April 1936) had previously announced the likely publication of the paper in April 1936.]

185. AL-DHIKRA
Singapore; thrice-monthly until January 1939, fortnightly from September 1939; [? 10 September] 1938–January 1939, 4 September 1939–[?]
Editor: Abdullah b. Abdul Rahman al-Habshi
Holdings:
BM*: Vol. I, Nos. 2–9 (Sept. 1938–Jan. 1939); Nos. 11–28 (Sept. 1939–May 1940)

[Note: There was a break in publication between issues No. 9 (possibly No. 10) in January 1939 and No. 11 (or possibly No. 10) in September or late August 1939.]

186. AL-AKHBAR
Singapore; daily until May 1940, thereafter weekly; 12 September 1939–May 1940, 21 June 1940–[? month] 1941
Editor: Sayyid A. W. Jilani
Holdings:
BM*: Vol. I, Nos. 1–100 (Sept. 1939–Jan. 1940); II, Nos. 1–100 (Jan.–May 1940); n.s. Vol. I, Nos. 1–6, 11–27 (June 1940–Jan. 1941); II, Nos. 28–51 (Jan.–July 1941); III, Nos. 52–8 (July–Aug. 1941)
UM*: Vol. I, Nos. 93–4, 96–100; II, Nos. 1–82

[Note: This paper had two separate existences, first as a daily and then (marked 'n.s.' here) as a weekly.]

187. AL-AKHBAR AL-MUSAWWARAH
Singapore; weekly; [? 8 July] 1939–[?]
Editor: Sayyid A. W. Jilani
Holdings:
UM*: Vol. I, Nos. 19–20 (Nov. 1940)

188. AL-ISLAH
Singapore; ? frequency; ? dates
Editor: Shaykh Karamah Baladran

Holdings:

[Note: The only known reference to this occurs in W. H. Ingrams's unpublished report on his visit to Malaya and Java in 1939, but no details are given. It is just possible that it is an early paper, published *c.* 1900–5, described by informants as a weekly, lithographed journal with a green cover, and possibly edited by Sayyid Mohammad Agil b. Yahya, assisted by Shaykh Karamah Baladran, and perhaps Sayyid Hassan b. Shahab, though there is also a possibility that the latter journal is being confused with the Malay-language *Al-Imam* (1906–9), with which Mohammad Agil was certainly associated.]

SECTION THREE: MISSIONARY

189. PUNGUTAN SEGALA REMAH PUNGATAUAN

Singapore; quarterly; March 1852–[? December 1852]
Editor:
Holdings:
BM*: Vol. I, Nos. 1–4 (Mar.–Dec. 1852)

[Note: This was a Christian mission publication, known in English as *The Malay Gleaner*.]

190. CHERMIN MATA

Singapore; ? frequency; [? 1857]–[?]
Editor:
Holdings:
BM*: Nos. 3 (Oct. 1858), 4 (? month 1859), 5 (? month 1859)

[Note: A lithographed, illuminated publication, concerning which most details of sponsorship are unclear, though it was probably the product of Christian mission activity. The extended title read 'Chermin mata bagi segala orang yang menuntut pengetahuan'.]

191. SAHABAT

Singapore; monthly; April 1895–[? March 1897], May 1902–March 1905, May 1905–[?]
Editor: Mrs. J. R. Denyes from May 1905
Holdings:
BM*: Vol. I, Nos. 1, 3–5 (Apr.–Aug. 1895); III, Nos. 1, 3, 5–7, 10–12 (May 1902–May 1903); IV, Nos. 1–4, 6–12 (June 1903–May 1904); V, Nos. 1–12 (June 1904–Mar. 1905); VI, Nos. 1/2/3 (May/July 1905), 8–13 (Dec. 1905–May 1906); VII, Nos. 1–7 (June–Dec. 1906)

[Note: A Methodist Mission publication. In Volume III, the issues for April and May 1903 are both numbered 12.]

192. PLAJARAN SKOLA AGAMA

Singapore; monthly; [? April 1896]–[?]
Editor:
Holdings:
BM*: Apr.–Dec. 1896; Feb., Apr.–Dec. 1899; Jan.–Dec. 1900; Jan.–Sept. 1901; Feb., July, Sept.–Dec. 1902; Mar.–July, Sept.–Dec. 1903; Jan.–Oct. 1904

[Note: A Christian-mission publication, containing weekly religious lessons. Issues were not numbered.]

193. WARTA MELAYU

Singapore; monthly; 23 March 1898–[?] (Rumi/English and Jawi editions)
Editor:
Holdings:
BM*: Vol. I, Nos. 1–12 (Mar. 1898–Feb. 1899) [Jawi edition]; Vol. I, Nos. 1–10 (Mar.–Dec. 1898) [Rumi/English edition]
AN*, UM°, US°: Vol. I, Nos. 1, 6 [Jawi edition]

[Note: A journal published by the American Mission in two separate editions, one Rumi and English, the other Jawi.]

194. PERTANDAAN ZAMAN

Singapore; monthly; [? 1912]–[?]
Editors: M. Munson; F. A. Detamore; Roger Altran
Holdings:
BM*: Vol. VIII, Nos. 1, 8–9 (Apr.–Dec. 1919); IX, Nos. 1, 3–6, 8–10, 12 (Jan.–Dec. 1920); X, Nos. 1–7, 9–12 (Jan.–Dec. 1921); XI, Nos. 1–2, 4–12 (Jan.–Dec. 1922); XII, Nos. 1–12 (Jan.–Dec. 1923); XIII, Nos. 1–12 (Jan.–Dec. 1924); XIV, Nos. 1–12 (Jan.–Dec. 1925); XV, Nos. 1–12 (Jan.–Dec. 1926); XVI, Nos. 1–12 (Jan.–Dec. 1927); XVII,

Nos. 1–12 (Jan.–Dec. 1928); XVIII, Nos. 1–4, 12 (Jan.–Apr., Dec. 1929); XIX, Nos. 1–9 (1930, undated]

[Note: A Christian mission journal.]

195. BOEKOE PELADJARAN SEKOLA SABAT
Singapore; quarterly; 3 January 1920–[?]
Editor:
Holdings:
BM*: Two unnumbered quarterly issues, Jan.–Mar. 1920, and July–Sept. 1920

[Note: Weekly Bible lessons, presumably, in view of the orthography, intended for Indonesian consumption.]

196. WARTA GEREDJA
Singapore, 1926–January 1929, then Bandung; monthly; January 1926–[?]

Editor: M. Munson
Holdings:
BM*: Vol. II, Nos. 1–12 (Jan. 1926–Dec. 1926); III, Nos. 1–12 (Jan.–Dec. 1927); IV, Nos. 1–12 (Jan.–Dec. 1928); V, Nos. 1–9 (Jan.–Sept. 1929)

[Note: A Seventh Day Adventist journal, presumably, in view of the orthography and later the place of publication, intended for Indonesian consumption.]

197. CHAHAYA
Singapore; monthly; January 1937–[?] (? Rumi)
Editor: Sutan Mengatas
Holdings:

[Note: This was apparently a Christian journal (? Seventh Day Adventist). The editor is thought to have been a Batak.]

SELECT BIBLIOGRAPHY

Ahmad *b. Nik* Hassan, *Nik*, 'The Malay Vernacular Press' (unpublished B.A. thesis, Department of History, University of Malaya in Singapore, 1958).

Ahmad Saleh, 'Peranan Suratkhabar dalam Perkembangan Sastera Melayu Moden' *Dewan Bahasa* (Kuala Lumpur), VI, 4 (1962), 164–9.

Ali *b. Haji* Ahmad, 'Ringkasan Riwayat Hidup Abdul Rahim Kajai, Ketua Pengarang *Malai Sinbun Sha*', *Dewan Bahasa*, III, 4 (1959), 161–70.

Birch, E. W., 'The Vernacular Press in the Straits', *Journal of the Royal Asiatic Society, Straits Branch*, 4 (1879), 51–5 [reprinted, *Journal of the Royal Asiatic Society, Malaysian Branch*, XLII (1969), 192–5].

Cheng Mong Hock, *The Early Chinese Newspapers of Singapore, 1881–1912* (Singapore, Oxford University Press, 1967).

Ghazali Ismail, *Tempat Jatoh Lagi Di-Kenang* (Singapore, Penerbitan Riwayah, n.d.).

Harun *b.* Abdul Karim, 'Malay Journalism in Malaya', *Merdeka Convention Papers* (London, 1957 [mimeograph]).

'Ibnu Haniffah' (pseud.), fourteen articles dealing historically with the Malay and Indonesian press, *Berita Minggu* (Kuala Lumpur), 27 May; 3, 10, 17, 24 June; 1, 8, 15, 29 July; 5, 12, 19 August; 2, 9 September 1962.

Ismail Hussein, 'Abdul Rahim Kajai', *Dewan Bahasa*, III, 2 (1959), 585–97.

Li Chuan Siu, *Ikhtisar Sejarah Kesusasteraan Melayu Baru, 1830–1845* (Kuala Lumpur, Pustaka Antara, 1966).

Lie, T. S., 'A Bird's-Eye View of the Development of Modern Malay Literature, 1921–1941', *Review of Indonesian and Malayan Affairs* (Sydney), II, 2 and 3 (1968), 11–27 and 1–15.

Lim, Pui Huen, P., *Newspapers Published in the Malaysian Area. With a Union List of Local Holdings* (Occasional Paper No. 2, Institute of Southeast Asian Studies, Singapore, 1970).

Makepeace, W., 'The Press', in A. Wright and H. A. Cartwright (eds.), *Twentieth Century Impressions of British Malaya* (London, Lloyds Great Britain Publishing Co. Ltd., 1908), 253–66.

Merican, Marina, 'Syed Sheikh Al-Hadi dan Pendapat2nya Mengenai Kemajuan Kaum Perempuan' (unpublished B.A. thesis, Department of Malay Studies, University of Malaya in Kuala Lumpur, 1961).

Muhammad *b. Dato*' Muda, 'Tarikh Akhbar2 dan Majallah2 Melayu Keluaran Semenanjong Tanah Melayu', *Majallah Guru*, XV, 10 (1938), 361–408.

—— *Tarikh Surat Khabar* (Bukit Mertajam, Matba'ah al-Zainiah, 1940).

Muhammad Taib *b.* Osman, *Bahasa Renchana Pengarang Akhbar2 hingga ka tahun 1941* (Kuala Lumpur, Dewan Bahasa & Pustaka, 1964) [published in English as *The Language of the Editorials in Malay Vernacular Newspapers up to 1941* (Kuala Lumpur, Dewan Bahasa & Pustaka, 1966)].

Muhammad Taif *b*. Osman, *An Introduction to the Development of Modern Malay Language and Literature* (Singapore, Eastern Universities Press, 1961).

Omar Mohd. Hashim, 'Perkembangan Cherpen Melayu sebelum Perang', *Dewan Bahasa*, v, 8 (1961), 343–56.

Roff, William R., *Guide to Malay Periodicals, 1876–1941. With details of known holdings in Malaya* (Papers on Southeast Asian Subjects No. 4, Singapore, Eastern Universities Press, 1961).

—— *Sejarah Surat2 Khabar Melayu* (Monograf Persekutuan Bahasa Melayu Universiti Malaya No. 1, Penang, Sinaran Press, 1967).

—— 'Indonesian and Malay Students in Cairo in the 1920s', *Indonesia* (Ithaca), 9 (1970), 73–87.

Tan Tat Seng, 'Sin Ma Wü Wen pao yeh pai nien shi' [One hundred years of Malay press in Singapore and Malaya], *Journal of Southeast Asian Researches* (Singapore), v (1969), 147–59 [with English summary].

Utusan Melayu Press, *Utusan Melayu 10 Tahun* (Singapore, 1949).

—— *Utusan Melayu 25 Tahun* (Kuala Lumpur, 1964).

Zabedah Awang Ngah, *Renongan: Antoloji Esei Melayu dalam tahun 1924–1941* (Kuala Lumpur, Dewan Bahasa & Pustaka, 1964).

Zainal Abidin *b*. Ahmad, 'Malay Journalism in Malaya', *Journal of the Royal Asiatic Society, Malayan Branch*, XIX, 2 (1941), 244–50.

Note: Much useful bibliographical and other relevant information may be obtained from many of the periodicals themselves. Particularly valuable in this respect are *Pengasoh* and *Al-Hikmah* (both published in Kota Bharu, Kelantan), which for many years printed notices of new publications and issues newly received. *Majallah Guru* is also a frequent source of information, especially concerning people.

ALPHABETICAL INDEX OF TITLES

(Roman figures indicate page numbers, italic item numbers.)

ALPHABETICAL INDEX OF PROPER NAMES

(PERSONS AND ORGANIZATIONS ASSOCIATED WITH THE PERIODICALS)

ALPHABETICAL INDEX BY STATE OF
PUBLICATION

(EXCLUDING SINGAPORE AND PENANG)